EXPLORING THE BOUNDARIES OF CONTRACT

Issues in Law and Society

General Editor: Michael Freeman

Titles in the Series:

Children's Rights: A Comparative Perspective
Edited by Michael Freeman

Divorce: Where Next?
Edited by Michael Freeman

Exploring the Boundaries of Contract
Edited by Roger Halson

Law as Communication
Edited by David Nelken

Iraqgate: The Constitutional Implications of the Matrix-Churchill Affairs
Edited by Rodney Austin

Positivism Today
Edited by Stephen Guest

Governing Childhood
Edited by Anne McGillivray

Exploring the Boundaries of Contract

Edited by

ROGER HALSON
Lecturer in Laws
University College London

Dartmouth

Aldershot • Brookfield USA • Singapore • Sydney

Published by
Dartmouth Publishing Company Limited
Gower House
Croft Road
Aldershot
Hants GU11 3HR
England

Dartmouth Publishing Company
Old Post Road
Brookfield
Vermont 05036
USA

British Library Cataloguing in Publication Data
Exploring the boundaries of contract. - (Issues in law and society)
   1. Contracts - Great Britain
   I. Series II. Halson, Roger
   344.1'062

Library of Congress Cataloging-in-Publication Data
Exploring the boundaries of contract / edited by Roger Halson.
      p.   cm. – (Issues in law and society)
   ISBN 1-85521-701-5 (hardcover). – ISBN 1-85521-712-0 (pbk.)
    1. Contracts–Great Britain. 2. Contracts–Social aspects.
  3. Contracts–Economic aspects. 4. Contracts–Moral and ethical
aspects. I. Halson, Roger. II. Series.
KD1554.E97   1996
346.41'02–dc20
[344.1062]   95-51300
                                              CIP

ISBN 1 85521 701 5 (Hbk)
ISBN 1 85521 712 0 (Pbk)

Printed in Great Britain by Galliard (Printers) Ltd, Great Yarmouth

Contents

Introduction

In varied senses the law of contract may be said to be fundamental. The doctrines that collectively comprise the law of contract ostensibly regulate much of the daily lives of citizens, form part of the compulsory diet fed to aspiring lawyers and the concept of a contract is utilised in moral and political philosophy. The subject clearly wants for definition. Yet this collection of essays aims only to suggest an inclusive definition. All the essays seek to explore the boundaries of contract but do so in diverse ways: some seek to explore issues of general theory, some reflect on empirical studies, some examine European influences, some address proposed reforms of the law and others the impact of particular contractual doctrines on other bodies of domestic law.

The terms "public" and "private" law are used to distinguish different areas of legal study. However questions can arise which concern the interaction between these two sets of principles. In the first essay Professor Sue Arrowsmith suggests that the courts have not paid sufficient attention to the proper relationship between these sets of principles to the detriment of the private interests of citizens.

The law of contract is, with the possible exception of land law, one of the last areas of domestic law to feel the influence of Europe. In the light of the Maastricht Treaty and the adoption of the principle of subsidiarity Professor Hugh Beale looks at different levels of "Europeanisation"; in particular he examines the problems that will have to be faced if that process is to be extended to the traditional domain of our doctrines of mistake and misrepresentation.

The case-law of contract may be said to reflect a tension between competing ideologies. In his essay Professor Roger Brownsword contrasts the ideologies of "consumer welfarism" and "market-individualism" and, by reference to recent decisions, elaborates a distinction between static and dynamic versions of market individualism.

Concepts which form part of the general law of contract are sometimes required to do valuable work in other contexts. Such, according to Professor Roger Rideout, is the case with the implied term doctrine as applied to contracts of employment where it offers a useful tool to control the employment relationship by the imposition of standards of reasonableness. However dangers may attend such applications. Professor Michael Freeman suggests that the time is ripe for a reconsideration of the doctrine associated with the case of *Balfour v Balfour* in order to permit a new assessment of the role of contract in intimate relationships.

Shortly after its creation the Law Commission recognised the primacy of contract by making its codification Item 1 of the first programme of law reform. Perhaps they paid even more eloquent testimony to the complexity of modern contract law by taking the decision to abandon the project.[1] However the Commission has been responsible for numerous proposed, and implemented, reforms of the law of contract. Perhaps one of the most fundamental is that proposed in their Consultation Paper on privity.[2] In my essay I argue that the Law Commission's failure to address the question "why do we enforce contracts?" means it is unable to resolve the difficulties posed by the competing interests of the third party and the original contractors when the latter propose an amendment to their contract.

Contract scholarship has in recent years displayed an increasing interest in empirical studies. Something more than intuition or anecdote about the real world has been demanded and this has been met by a small number of empirical studies which have enjoyed an influence beyond their number.[3] In his essay Professor Norman Palmer draws upon a piece of research in a rarely examined context, loans of works of art.

It can be seen that the essays which follow are catholic and wide-ranging. It is hoped that the reader will also find them to be enjoyable and informative.

ROGER HALSON

Notes

1. 8th Annual Report 1972-3, Law Comm. No 58, paras 3-4.
2. No 121 (1991) *Privity of Contract: Contracts for the Benefit of Third Parties.*
3. E.g. Macaulay (1963) 28 Am. Soc. Rev. 55 and Beale and Dugdale(1975) 2 B.J.L.S. 45.

1 The Impact of Public Law on the Private Law of Contract

SUE ARROWSMITH

Introduction

English law does not make a formal conceptual distinction between "public law" and "private law", but these terms are used in practice to describe particular areas of legal study. "Public law" is used in a broad sense to refer to the constitutional and legal principles relating to the organisation and responsibility of government, whilst the term "private law" covers, *inter alia*, the legal rules governing the relationships of individuals under the law of obligations - that is, the law of contract, tort and restitution. Since, however, the government is in principle subject to the ordinary "private" law of obligations, the relations of government in this area can raise issues of interest to both public and private lawyers.

The inter-relationship between the "private" law of contract and public law in its broadest sense has numerous aspects, many of which have been the subject of academic debate. One issue, for example, is whether private contract law has any utility at all as a framework for ordering certain types of relationships involving public, or quasi public, bodies.[1] This has been considered, for example, in the context of the relationship between providers of public services such as gas, water and postal services, and the recipients of those services;[2] and between government agencies providing grants and subsidies and the recipients.[3] How far should these relationships, which do not in general have any parallel in dealings conducted between ordinary private persons, be construed as contractual, rather than as based purely on rights and obligations imposed by legislation? Until recently there was even some doubt as to whether the relationship of the Crown with its servants - which does have an obvious parallel with private relationships - should be treated as contractual;

3

but it is now generally acknowledged that the relationship is a contractual one.[4] Another aspect of public contracting is the extent to which legal and constitutional controls over government activity - such as the principles of judicial review or control by the "Ombudsmen" - should apply to government when it is engaged in contractual activities.[5] The author has argued elsewhere that in general the application of such principles is not rendered inappropriate by the existence of, or intention to create, a private contractual agreement to govern the relationship: it is normally desirable to apply such "public law "doctrines alongside relevant rules of private law.[6]

Consideration of these issues, as well as others such as the details of legislative rules regulating government procurement procedures, or the constitutional use of contract to achieve social objectives, has generally been the province of public lawyers - those interested in constitutional and administrative law - rather than of "private", contract, lawyers. This is not surprising since the issues raised are mainly those of constitutional organisation and accountability, rather than the policy and analytical concerns familiar to contract lawyers. A detailed consideration of such issues is thus - quite appropriately - omitted from most contract law texts. However, there is one major area of concern in government contracting where both "public" and "private" law approaches and techniques must be applied in order to achieve a satisfactory resolution of legal problems. This is the situation where it is acknowledged that special public law rules - derived either from legislation or the common law - *do* regulate the formation or termination of a contract, and it is necessary to determine what the consequences of those rules are to be for private contractual liability.

One topical aspect of this problem is the effect on private contractual liability of a breach of public law rules governing the making of a contract. Such rules may relate either to the subject matter of contracts, or to the procedures or formalities for their conclusion. The effect of rules restricting the subject matter of public contracts was raised as an important practical issue following the recent litigation in *Hazell v Hammersmith and Fulham L.B.C.*[7] concerning unlawful "interest rate swap" transactions, and has subsequently also been considered by the High Court in a different context in the decisions in *Credit Suisse v Allerdale B.C.*[8] and *Morgan Grenfell v London Borough of Sutton.*[9] As regards the effect of formal or procedural restrictions, this has not been as significant in English law as in some other jurisdictions, since the government has generally shied away from legal regulation of contract procedures. However, it has become more important with the adoption of recent legislation to regulate the award of major procurement contracts under European Community law.

It will be suggested in this essay that in deciding these questions concerning the impact of public law on the private law of contract the courts, as in other contexts, have not given adequate consideration to the proper relationship between public law and private law principles. In this particular context, this

4

has resulted in inadequate protection for the private interests of citizens.

Restrictions on the subject matter of contracts

The principle of limited contract power

The Crown possesses all the powers of natural persons, including the power to contract, and thus may enter into contracts for any purpose without Parliamentary authorisation.[10] However, government bodies created by statute, a category which includes most local authorities, possess only the powers conferred upon them by their enabling legislation,[11] and thus may enter into contracts only to the extent permitted by that legislation.[12] Thus, for example, if the legislation does not permit a particular authority to operate a leisure centre, should it decide to do so contracts made in connection with the centre - for example, a contract for its construction - are unlawful.

This principle was recently, and controversially, applied by the House of Lords in *Hazell v Hammersmith and Fulham L.B.C.*[13] The case concerned "interest rate swap" transactions, which were a type of speculative financial transaction entered into by a number of local authorities in the 1980s. In the *Hammersmith* case itself the transactions would result in a profit for the authority if interest rates moved down, but a loss if they should rise. Rates rose significantly and the authority stood to lose a sum amounting to several times its annual budget if the contracts were enforceable against it. The auditor sought a declaration to determine whether the contracts were lawful. The House of Lords held that they were not, since no legislative authority could be found for local authorities to engage in transactions of this type.[14] This case makes it clear that local authorities have no power to enter into an interest rate swap transaction in any circumstances, and thus all contracts of this type are unlawful. However, many transactions are of a type which are capable of being lawful, but which are unlawful because of the purpose for which they are made in the particular case. Thus a contract for the purchase of computer equipment will be lawful if the equipment is intended for use in connection with the authority's lawful functions, but not if it is purchased specifically for a project which is itself *ultra vires*.

The legal consequences of an unlawful agreement: the approach of the courts[15]

The application of this doctrine of limited contract power is straightforward in principle (although not always easy to apply in practice). More difficult is the question of the legal consequences of an unlawful agreement. There are three distinct questions: whether the agreement may be enforced by the authority;[16] whether it may be enforced against that authority; and whether it may be challenged by a third party.

As to the first, the House of Lords held in *Ashbury Carriage and Iron Co. v Riche*[17] that an unlawful agreement concluded by a private statutory corporation - to which the same principles of limited contract power apply - could not be enforced *against* the corporation. Having concluded that the agreement was not permitted, their Lordships did not give detailed consideration to the consequences[18] and simply assumed that it was "void" in the sense of being devoid of any legal effect. It was subsequently assumed that this principle would apply also to unlawful agreements by public bodies.[19] Following the decision of the House of Lords in *Hammersmith v Hazell,* holding that there was no legislative basis for interest rate swap transactions, it was thus generally accepted by those involved that the transactions could not be enforced against the authorities concerned.[20] Thus the question of enforceability of the contracts was not raised in subsequent litigation, which dealt merely with the restitutionary and proprietary aspects of the transactions.

It can be noted, however, that the *Hammersmith* case itself did not deal with enforceability. The case had concerned an application by the authority's auditor for a declaration that the actions of the council were unlawful, and the House limited itself to a declaration to this effect, without examining the legal effects of the unlawful transactions. Since there was no other clear authority in English law for the view that contracts with *public* bodies are unenforceable it appeared open to those who had engaged in swap transactions with local authorities to argue that these could nevertheless be enforced, but surprisingly this was not done.

However, the issue has now been considered in two recent High Court decisions concerning different types of unlawful agreements, and in these cases the courts have specifically ruled that unlawful agreements are invalid. In the first, *Credit Suisse v Allerdale B.C.,*[21] a local authority sought to build a swimming pool for the local population but was unable to finance the project without exceeding its borrowing limits. These it sought to evade by setting up a company to carry out the project and take out the loan, the council guaranteeing the loan. The company also undertook the development of time shares with the intention that the sale of these would provide finance for the pool. The time shares failed to generate the expected revenue, however, and the company collapsed. The authority claimed that its own guarantee of the loan could not be enforced on the basis that the guarantee agreement was unlawful. Colman J held the agreement of guarantee was indeed unlawful, both because it was entered into for an improper purpose (to evade the restrictions on local authority borrowing requirements) and because it was "tainted" by the time share project which was wholly outside the authority's powers. Having concluded that the guarantee was unlawful, the judge considered arguments that unlawful agreements are enforceable against the authority in some

6

circumstances.[22] Ultimately, however, he concluded that such agreements are unenforceable, and that exceptions cannot be made. The same view was endorsed by Clarke J in the later case of *Morgan Grenfell v London Borough of Sutton*,[23] which concerned an unlawful council guarantee of a loan made by the bank to a housing association and an unlawful agreement to indemnify the housing association for losses in connection with a particular housing scheme. In this case, also, the effects of an unlawful agreement were examined, and the judge held that neither agreement was enforceable against the council.

If this view is correct, it is clear that (at least where the authority has not already performed its own part)[24] the authority itself cannot enforce the other party's promise since, the authority's own promise being unenforceable, there is no consideration. Further, if such an agreement has no legal effect between the parties it will be open to challenge by way of judicial review by a third party who has standing, such as a taxpayer or ratepayer complaining of unlawful local authority spending.

Critique of the courts' approach

It may be questioned, however, whether the solution adopted in *Ashbury* and *Allerdale* is appropriate.

First, it should be pointed out that the fact that a contract is not permitted need not automatically entail the conclusion that it is devoid of legal consequences. This was simply assumed in *Ashbury*[25] and Colman J in *Allerdale* was led to his conclusion by similar "conceptual" reasoning, explicitly rejecting an approach based on "policy" in favour of the conclusion that absence of "capacity" dictated the result that the transaction was devoid of legal effect in private law.[26] However, in general there is no reason why an act which is not permitted may not have legal consequences if carried out. As was pointed out by Warren as far back as 1926, in considering the *Ashbury* decision, "To say that a corporation *has* disregarded the limits on its powers is to beg the fundamental question whether it has legal capacity to act...".[27] That acts in breach of public law may be fully effective can be seen, for example, in the fact that many procedural restrictions in legislation are construed by the courts so as not to affect the validity of acts done in contravention of the restriction. In many of these cases the restriction is construed not to invalidate *any* acts or decisions concluded in contravention of the statute, but in the case of procedural rules affecting contract awards - as is explained in the text below - it has sometimes been provided expressly, or implied by the courts, that the restriction may invalidate acts leading to the award of the contract, but not the actual conclusion of the contract, so that that act is effective for the purpose of creating private law rights. There is no reason why the same approach should not be adopted in construing the effect of restrictions on the subject matter of contracts. An analogy for applying this approach where the subject matter of a contract is prohibited is found in *Sutton's Hospital* case.[28] In this case it was

7

held that a corporation created by charter under the Crown's common law powers may be restrained for making a contract outside the terms of its charter, but that, once concluded, such a contract is effective.

In determining the consequences of a contract made in breach of public law, a careful analysis is needed of the policy arguments for and against particular legal consequences, in light of the nature of the particular transaction.[29] This is the kind of analysis which has been carried out by the courts in the context of contracts affected by breaches of legal restrictions which constitute a legal wrong or by other legal rules of "public policy", which are generally grouped together under the heading of "illegal contracts".[30] Several policy issues arise.

The first is whether it is directly contrary to the policy of the prohibition to give the requested remedy for the specific transaction. In practice, most of the restrictions on public bodies' power to make contracts are concerned to prevent the authority's funds being used at all for certain activities or to prevent public funds being put at risk (in particular, through trading activities or speculative financial deals, as in *Hammersmith*). In this case to enforce the contract by requiring the authority to pay for goods or services received, or to require payment of damages for failure to go ahead with the transaction, would contravene the objectives of the restrictions on contract power. However, it is difficult to see that this public interest should outweigh the interest which the other party has under private law contract principles. It is generally accepted that there is liability in tort for actions of the authority which are *ultra vires*[31] or which are carried out in the course of ultra vires activity[32] - and, indeed, it might be said that any tort is outside the authority's powers. If it is appropriate to allow public funds to be used to compensate tort victims even though this does not involve expenditure "properly" incurred by the authority to promote the general public interest, it is difficult to see why contractual rights should not in general be similarly protected, at least where the contractor did not, and should not, have known that the agreement was unlawful.

A second concern, which has influenced the courts in relation to other types of unlawful agreement, is the need to deter such agreements. It might be argued that unlawful agreements with public bodies should be held unenforceable, so that contractors concluding an agreement with public bodies have an incentive to check that the agreement is permitted under the relevant legislation. However, in practice public authorities themselves are in general in a much better position than contractors to do this. This suggests that a more appropriate rule is to require payment of damages where the agreement turns out to be unlawful, so placing the incentive to comply on the authority, except where the contractor knows or should have known of the restrictions. Further, an additional argument for this approach, as pointed out by Cane, is that to place the risk of *ultra vires* on contractors may discourage them from doing business with government and at the very least increase the cost of the transactions, which must be priced to take account of the risk.[33]

These arguments suggest the conclusion, put forward previously by this author and also by other writers,[34] that in general, agreements which exceed the restrictions on a corporation's contract power should not render the agreement wholly unenforceable, unless the contractor knew,[35] or perhaps should have known, of the breach of the restriction. A similar solution has been provided by statute for private companies incorporated under the Companies Acts[36] and also for contracts of loan with local authorities, which may be enforced by the lender even when not authorised by statute.[37] The *Hammersmith* case appears something of a "hard case" since the consequences of the loss if the contract was enforceable against the authority were unusually large (as indicated above, several times its annual budget); but such hard cases will be unusual and should not affect the development of the general principle. It is interesting that both Colman J in *Allerdale* and Clarke J in *Morgan Grenfell* expressed support for this approach as a matter of policy. However, in *Allerdale*, as noted above, the judge appeared to take the view that an act which is "void" in public law cannot have legal effect in private law, whilst in *Morgan Grenfell*, the judge indicated that he considered it beyond his own proper role to overturn the accepted assumption that unlawful public contracts are unenforceable: whether the existing "common law rule" should be changed was, he said, "matter of policy" for Parliament, and he preferred to follow the approach already established in *Allerdale*. This is an unnecessarily conservative view of the judge's role. Since there was no clear authority of a higher court to establish the invalidity of the agreement, and the private law cases offering an analogy appear to be based on fallacious reasoning, it would have been quite appropriate for the judge to reach a different conclusion based on his own view of the desirable solution to this type of problem.

Whilst the other party should be able to obtain damages for non-performance, it does not necessarily follow, on the other hand, that specific performance or an injunction will be given, even in circumstances where such remedies would be granted were the contract lawful - for example, to enforce a sale of land which the authority is forbidden to sell. Such remedies are discretionary, and it is likely that where the authority's performance involves a prohibited act the court would recognise that it may refuse relief. It is far from clear that specific relief must always be refused, however; the best approach would be to balance the nature and importance of the public law restriction against the need to protect the plaintiff.

So far as the authority is concerned, it is not appropriate to allow that body to enforce an unlawful executory agreement, since this would be quite clearly contrary to the policy of the statute. Thus, to this extent the private law relationship should be regarded as "vitiated" by the breach of public law.

If, as advocated above, the court should take the view that the contract may be enforced against the authority in some circumstances, the question arises as to the position of a third party with standing to challenge the decision in judicial proceedings. There is no reason why the third party should not be permitted to challenge decisions leading up to the contract - for example, to quash a decision

9

that such a contract should be put out to tender, or to seek an injunction to prevent the authority from making such a contract. On the other hand, if the breach of the public law restriction does not wholly vitiate the parties' private law contractual obligations, it is inappropriate to allow an action attacking the contract in general. Thus the court should not, for example, award *certiorari* to quash the contract, or declare it void. However, it seems clear that the authority must be under a public law duty not to proceed with any transaction which it has improperly made except as required to so do to fulfil its private law obligations, and that this duty may be enforced by third parties. Thus, for example, it is submitted that such a party could obtain an injunction to prevent the authority from allowing a contractor to proceed with construction work under an unlawful contract, or from delivering under a contract an object of which the sale is prohibited, unless the circumstances are such that a court would order specific performance of the contract to protect the contractor's interest. This approach will require the judge in a judicial review action to apply private law contract principles; but this is unobjectionable, and, indeed, essential if the necessary consistency is to be maintained between public and private law.

The other party to the contract may also wish to challenge the agreement by way of judicial review, and since his private rights are affected will be given standing to do so.[38] Such a party, like a third party, is presumably able to challenge decisions leading up to the agreement to make it clear that it is unlawful, and also to restrain the authority from breaching its public law duties not to proceed with the agreement. However, since the agreement itself is not wholly without legal effect, in that it may give rise to contractual rights, it should not be possible to quash the contract as such.

In *Allerdale* counsel for the bank contemplated a relationship between the principles applied in private law and those in judicial review proceedings, but in a different form from that suggested above. In that case it was argued that the contractual position should be determined by considering whether or not the court would invalidate the agreement in judicial review proceedings. Since the court has a discretion to refuse a remedy in review proceedings, an approach linking private law rules to judicial review would give rise to the possibility of the court's refusing to deny the enforceability of the contract in private law as well. Counsel argued that this discretion to refuse a remedy should be exercised in public law where the other party is ignorant of the government's breach; and hence that the invalidity of the contract should also be denied in a private law action in such circumstances.

It is submitted, however, that this argument approaches the issue from the wrong direction: the better approach is that the position in public law actions is determined by the general principles governing the enforceability of contracts. This is because the contractual position should be defined as a matter of right, and not subject to the wide-ranging discretion which the court enjoys in public law cases. In particular, in judicial review actions there the courts

10

enjoy a discretion to refuse relief on a variety of grounds; but - as was recognised in *Allerdale* - private law claims, even against public bodies, are not subject to such discretionary limitations. For example, a claim for misfeasance in public office based on the fact that the government has knowingly acted in an unlawful manner may be brought without first challenging the decision by way of judicial review,[39] and such a claim also will not be defeated by the fact that the court would not have exercised its discretion to quash the decision in proceedings for judicial review, had the invalidity been raised in that procedure. The argument of counsel was rightly rejected by the judge for this reason, namely, the absence of the existence of discretionary grounds for denying relief in private law proceedings. However, as argued above, he should have recognised the enforceability of the authority's obligations in certain circumstances as a matter of private law. In other words, the rule that an innocent party may enforce the contract in certain circumstances is not subject to any discretion of the court to deny the possibility. On this approach the rule that a third party may not challenge the contract itself in public law proceedings, nor obtain any remedy which would have the effect of denying relief in contract in the public law action itself, also arises from the general principle that the breach of public law does not vitiate the contract: it does not derive from the existence or exercise of any public law discretion to deny legal effect to the contract in a judicial review action.

Rules on contract procedures and formalities

Procedures and formalities in English law

Legislation sometimes prescribes certain procedures or formalities for the conclusion of contracts. Some of these are designed at least partly to control the process for deciding on a particular transaction (for example, whether the authority should construct a library, or enter into interest rate swaps transaction). This was the case, for example, with certain common law and statutory requirements which formerly existed in the United Kingdom for corporate public bodies to affix the corporate seal to contracts. However, the author is not aware of any current requirements of this kind. More often, procedural requirements are concerned with efficiency in concluding a transaction, and in preventing corruption. For example, tendering requirements, or requirements for works contracts to be approved at a particular level in the administrative hierarchy, may be set in order to ensure that the cheapest or best value contractor is employed to build a particular work. Many countries have extensive legislation to promote these objectives for procurement contracts, but the United Kingdom has traditionally relied on administrative and political controls thus largely avoiding the potential conflict between legal regulation and private law liability. However, there has always been some legislation in this area, as noted below. Further, in the last few

11

years detailed regulations have been adopted to regulate the award of major procurement contracts, in the form of the Public Works Contracts Regulations 1991,[40] Public Services Contracts Regulations 1993,[41] Public Supply Contracts Regulations 1995[42] and Utilities Contracts Regulations 1995,[43] which implement European Community directives designed to open up government and utilities procurement to fair Europe-wide procurement.[44]

In addition to these and other rules in legislation, the impact of a breach of public law on a contract may also arise where there is a breach of general administrative law principles. For example, in *R v Shell ex parte Lewisham L.B.C.*,[45] the court held that a decision to exclude firms from local authority contracts because of their business dealings in South Africa where taken with the motive of hastening the end of apartheid was unlawful as made for an improper purpose. Whilst the legality of specific contract awards was not in issue, clearly if Shell had protested at its exclusion from a particular contract the question would have been raised of the effect of the breach of public law on the contract.

The effect of a breach

Enforcement against the authority Where there is a breach of a procedural or formal requirement, it will generally be contrary to the policy of the rule breached to enforce the contract against the authority. For example, to enforce a contract made in breach of tendering requirements designed to secure value for money means that the authority is held to a contract which may not offer the best value. However, the case for upholding the policy of the rule above the private interest of the other party is generally not as strong here as where the subject matter of the contract is wholly forbidden, both in terms of the balance of public and private interests, and the deterrent to breach. Further, many breaches may not have any adverse impact on the public interest in practice - as where breach of tendering formalities would not have affected the choice of contractor.[46]

Where the matter is not governed by express provisions, a number of older cases have held that a breach of procedural requirements relating to procurement *does* affect a contract to the extent that the public authority itself may refuse to go ahead.[47] However, in other Commonwealth jurisdictions recent decisions have tended to favour the view that breach does not generally affect the other party's ability to enforce the contract.[48] It is submitted that, as with breaches relating to the subject matter of a contract, unless the legislation states to the contrary, breach of procedural provisions should not affect the other party's financial claims.[49] This approach should be applied, for example, in determining the effect of section 17 of the Local Government Act 1988, which prohibits local authorities from taking into account "non-commercial" considerations in their procurement, and also with breaches of general administrative law requirements.

Where the other party is aware of the breach, on the other hand, it may be acceptable to make an exception to allow the authority to renounce the contract. Such a principle will help to deter agreements made in breach of the rules and will also enable the public authority to reconsider the award decision in accordance with the proper procedures, if appropriate, in order to uphold the public interest.

In contrast with the case where there is a breach of rules restricting the subject matter of the contract, however, where it was suggested above that there is a duty on the authority to renounce the transaction where it is not fully enforceable by the other party, there may be some debate over whether it is appropriate in the case of a procedural breach to place the authority under a duty not to proceed. This is because the detriment to the public interest resulting from breach of a procedural requirement may well be outweighed by the inconvenience of commencing a new procedure, so that the best solution on balance may be to proceed with the agreement. This might indicate that the authority should enjoy a discretion over whether to proceed with the agreement, rather than being under a duty to do so. This question of whether public inconvenience should override the strict principle of legality is a difficult one, which also arises in judicial review cases. Here the difficulty is dealt with largely through time limits: it is required that applications for leave for judicial review must be made[50] within three months, and must also be made "promptly".[51] Whilst these time limits may be extended for "good reason",[52] relief may be refused in such cases of extension where this would be detrimental to good administration. It is not clear, on the other hand, whether there is a general discretion to refuse relief on grounds of administrative inconvenience at the trial in cases where proceedings are brought within the time limits stated above.[53] Whatever the position, however, it is clear that the solution adopted in considering the enforceability of the agreement between the parties should be consistent with the approach taken in judicial review cases.

One possible approach to enforceability in the case where the other party knows of the breach is to say that the authority *is* under a duty to renounce the transaction on the basis that illegality always overrides administrative convenience. This would only be logical if the courts are generally prepared to take such an approach in all timely judicial review cases, denying themselves a right to consider administrative convenience in such cases. However, even if this were to be the preferred attitude in judicial review, it can be pointed out that in judicial review the time limits for challenge are short, and that they have no application between the parties to the contract. It does not seem desirable to require the authority to renounce an agreement whenever the authority realises that the agreement is unlawful, which may happen a long time after the agreement is concluded. Thus it is submitted that this solution should be rejected.

The better view, then, is that the authority does enjoy some discretion in weighing up the different public interests involved, and in deciding whether to go ahead. However, it is submitted that it is not acceptable for the authority to renounce the agreement for reasons unconnected with the rule which has been breached in making the agreement - for example, because the market price of goods purchased under the agreement has dropped in the meantime. It is suggested that general administrative law principles, which requires that all administrative powers be exercised for proper purposes, will apply to ensure that the contract is rescinded only to protect the interest behind the rule which has been infringed. If this is correct, the private law position may best be summarised by saying that the contract is enforceable by a private party who is aware of the breach, but is subject to renunciation by the authority on grounds of public interest.

In some cases the effect of a breach of procedural rules on the contract is expressly dealt with by statute. In these cases the legislature has generally provided for the contract to be enforceable by the non-governmental party.[54] Thus section 135 of the Local Government Act 1972, which requires local authorities to adopt standing orders providing for competitive tendering, states that breach of the standing orders does not affect the validity of a subsequent contract and section 41(6) of the Fair Employment (Northern Ireland) Act 1989 provides that a breach of authorities' obligations not to contract with firms who are debarred for failure to meet their statutory "fair employment" obligations, which are concerned to eliminate inequalities of opportunity based on religion, does not invalidate any contract. In these cases it appears that the knowledge of the non-governmental party is immaterial to his ability to enforce his private rights.

The regulations implementing the European Community directives on procurement state expressly that once the contract has been concluded the only remedy available to a third party is damages.[55] However, the legislation does not state what is the effect of the agreement as between the parties. It is submitted, however, that it should follow from the rule which bars a challenge to the contract by a third party that the contract may be enforced against the authority: as is argued below, in all cases where the transaction is *not* fully enforceable against the authority it is logical that it should be open to attack by a third party. This approach is consistent with the general principle advocated above for the case where there is no express legislation, that where the other party does not know of the breach he should be able to enforce the contract.

Under the regulations there is probably an implied exception to the general rule that a third party may not challenge a concluded contract, to allow a challenge where the other party to the contract is aware that there has been a breach of the rules.[56] In this case there should also be an exception to the principle that the other party may enforce the contract, since if the contract *were* fully enforceable a third party challenge should not be allowed.

Enforcement by the authority The question also arises of the position where the public authority seeks to enforce the contract but the other party does not wish to go ahead. Where the subject matter of the contract is unlawful it is clear, as explained above, that the authority is obliged to stop the transaction. However, this need not be the case where there is no objection to the transaction as such but only to the method of formation. Here it is submitted that it should be for the authority to determine the balance between, on the one hand, the public interest behind the rule which has been breached and, on the other, the inconvenience which would arise if the contract were reconsidered, and that the private party should not be permitted to avoid its obligations simply for convenience; thus the authority should in all cases be able to proceed if it wishes to do so. (If it does not, then of course the parties may terminate the contract by mutual agreement). This is the position with the local authority tendering rules and "fair employment" legislation which make it clear that the contract is wholly effective and may not be renounced by the non-governmental party.

On the other hand, it could be argued that to allow the other party to decline to proceed will act as a deterrent to breaches of the law, and that this should be allowed at the very least, where the authority itself was (or perhaps should have been) aware of the breach.

Challenges to the contract by way of judicial review Challenges to a breach of procedural rules may come from third parties, especially those who hoped to obtain the contract themselves.

Where the contract is fully enforceable by the non-governmental party then, it is submitted, a third party should never be permitted to challenge the contract as such: the interest of the other contracting party should be protected against a third party challenge as well as against possible renunciation by the government. This is clearly the position under section 135 of the Local Government Act 1972 and under the "fair employment" legislation. Here the contract is wholly immune from challenge, including by third parties. However, decisions leading up to the contract may be subject to review.[57]

As noted above, third parties are also generally unable to challenge a contract made in breach of the Community procurement rules. However, whilst this is stated as a general principle in the regulations, and also in the directives which are implemented by these provisions,[58] it is possible that such a limitation on remedies may not be maintained where the non-regulated party is aware of the breach, under the general Community law requirement that "effective" remedies must be provided to enforce Community rules.[59]

As explained above, a similar principle - that the contract may generally be enforced by the other party, but may potentially be renounced by the authority where the other party is aware of the breach - is probably to be applied for breach of procedural rules where the legislation is silent on their effects. In these cases, where the other party does not know of the breach and may enforce the contract, it should again not be open to challenge by a third party.

Where the other party *does* know of the breach, it was suggested above that the authority may, if it chooses, renounce the contract. Even in this case it might be argued that it should not be open to challenge by a third party, on the basis that the authority decides whether the public interest requires the contract to proceed. In this the position would be different from that applying to a contract with an unlawful subject matter, where, since the authority has a duty not to go ahead, the contract is subject to third party review. The better view, however, is that in the absence of any express indication to the contrary, the contract may in this case be challenged by a third party, and that the question of whether a remedy should be refused on grounds of public inconvenience is a matter for the discretion of the court. In practice, interim relief will be needed to ensure that the contract is not already completed by the time of the trial and the courts have in fact indicated that they will refuse interim relief to hold up the contract where this would cause serious inconvenience to the public.[60]

Conclusion

In considering the effect of a breach of public law upon a contract the courts have taken the view that such a breach renders the contract wholly "void" and unenforceable. Decisions have generally been based on a simple assumption that acts categorised as "void" in public law cannot be effective to create rights in private law, but there is nothing to compel this conclusion. It has been argued above that, in general, priority should be given to the private interests reflected in the general rules of contract law. This means, in particular, that the other party to the contract who does not know that a breach of public law has occurred should be able to claim damages for breach of contract, although the public interest may sometimes require the court to deny specific performance or an injunction. This policy of favouring private interests has been adopted in legislation imposing procedural requirements, which has generally provided that contracts shall not be invalidated by a breach, without even making an exception where the other party is aware of the breach. To the extent that the contract *is* enforceable, this policy reflected in the private law of contract must then be carried through to judicial review actions, as explained. Where the other party does not know of the breach this will generally mean that the contract itself cannot be challenged, although it may be possible to challenge a public authority's actions leading up to the contract, and also any decision to proceed with the contract when this would be in breach of the authority's public law duties.

In the author's view this area of law provides merely one illustration of a more frequent failure by the courts to analyse in a systematic way the inter-relationship between public and private law in cases which concern the impact of public law rules on private rights. Other areas where this is seen are in the rule preventing fettering of discretion by contract, where the courts have held - inappropriately - that the contract is void *ab initio;*[61] the impact of the rule which prohibits the Crown from fettering its discretion to dismiss its servants, which denies to the servant all the ordinary remedies of contract law when dismissed in the public interest;[62] and cases on ostensible authority, holding that such authority may not exist where this would be contrary to some statutory provision.[63] The decisions in all these areas have been criticised by academic writers for the lack of sophistication in their reasoning, which has contributed to a situation where private rights and interests are afforded inadequate protection. Another illustration is seen in cases where public law remedies have been sought to challenge a decision to terminate an employment contract, where that decision has been made in breach of public law. Here it has been simply assumed that such remedies will have the effect of reinstating the applicant, on the grounds that the dismissal is "void"; but this appears inconsistent with the private law rule that specific performance of a contractual relationship will only be ordered in limited circumstances.[64] In this case, failure to properly examine both public and private law aspects of the case produces a result which favours the citizen against the state.

Instead of the simplistic approach which has often been adopted in the past, what is required in all cases of this kind is a careful evaluation of the different public and private interests involved, and of the existing public and private law principles, to produce a solution which takes proper account of both. In the case of contracts affected by public law restrictions concerning either the subject matter of the contract or the procedures for their conclusion, it is hoped that in future decisions the courts will depart from the unsophisticated view that equates "unlawful" with "void", and will engage in a more careful scrutiny of the policy issues involved. Whilst a change of approach will not inevitably lead to a reversal of the practical solutions adopted in previous cases, it has been argued here that a fair balance between the interests protected by "public" law and those reflected in the private law of contract does indeed demand a different result in the context of the cases considered in this essay.

Notes

1. See S.Arrowsmith, *Civil Liability and Public Authorities* (1992; Hull, Earlsgate Press), pp. 45-53.
2. See Foulkes, *Administrative Law* (7th ed. 1990; London, Butterworths), pp.432-8.
3. See Arrowsmith, supra.
4. See Craig, *Administrative Law* (3rd ed. 1994; London, Sweet & Maxwell), pp.707-9.

5.   See S.Arrowsmith, "Government Contracts and Public Law" (1990) 10 L.S. 231; B.V. Harris, "The Third Source of Authority for Government Action" (1992) 108 L.Q.R. 626; S. Arrowsmith, *Government Procurement and Judicial Review* (1988; Toronto, Carswell); S. Arrowsmith, "Judicial Review and the Contractual Powers of Public Authorities" (1990) 106 L.Q.R. 277.

6.   See the works cited in note 5 supra.

7.   [1992] 2 A.C. 1.

8.   Judgement of 6 May 1994.

9.   The Times, March 23 1995.

10.   *The Bankers Case* (1700) 90 E.R. 270; *J.E.Verrault & Fils v Quebec* [1977] 1 S.C.R. 41.

11.   *Attorney General v Manchester Corporation* [1906] 1 Ch. 643; *Attorney General v Fulham Corporation* [1921] 1 Ch. 44.

12.   *Hazell v Hammersmith and Fulham L.B.C.* [1992] 2 A.C. 1. Hammersmith itself had been created by charter issued pursuant to statute, but its contract powers were held to be restricted on the basis that the statute permitted such charter corporations to be given only the same powers as statutory corporations.

13.   [1991] 1 All E.R. 545.

14.   As indicated above, Hammersmith itself was an authority created by charter, but enjoyed exactly the same powers as statutory authorities.

15.   See also Warren, "Torts by Corporations in Ultra Vires Undertakings" (1926) 2 C.L.J. 180; Goodhart, "Corporate Liability in Tort and the Doctrine of Ultra Vires" (1926) 2 C.L.J. 350; S.Arrowsmith, *Civil Liability and Public Authorities*, supra, pp.62-5; P.Cane, (1994) 110 L.Q.R. 521 (case note).

16.   This question will generally arise in a private law action by the authority to enforce the agreement, but the other party may also be able to bring an action by way of judicial review to challenge the agreement, as to which see the text below.

17.   (1875) L.R. 7 H.L. 653.

18.   The only issue argued and considered was whether a "void" and unenforceable agreement could be ratified - not whether an unlawful agreement should be regarded as unenforceable in the first place.

19.   It was applied, for example, by the Supreme Court of Canada in *Sydney v Chappel Bros.* [1910] 43 S.C.R.478, and also in English cases which are unlawful as involving a fetter on discretion and procedural breaches of public law (discussed further below).

20.   See, for example, the statement of Dillon L.J. in *Westdeutsche Bank v Islington L.B.C.* [1994] 1 W.L.R. 938, at 943 that "Since *Hazell's* case was brought against the local authority by the district auditor, the courts did not have to decide the effect of the transaction having been ultra vires and void". This assumes that the case *did* decide that

the transaction was "void" in the sense of unenforceable, and that the matter remaining for the court in the *Islington* case was simply the restitutionary and property claims arising because of the invalidity of the transaction. However, as argued in the text, the *Hammersmith* case did not even decide the issue of enforceability.

21. Judgement of 6 May 1994.
22. One of these arguments, based on the existence of a discretion to award remedies in public law proceedings, which counsel suggested should be carried over to private law proceedings, is considered in the text below. The other argument was based on an analogy with company law, the reasoning of which does not, however, seem appropriate in the present context: see further Cane, supra.
23. The Times March 23 1995.
24. As to the position where the authority has already performed see S.Arrowsmith, *Government Procurement and Judicial Review* (1988; Toronto, Carswell),
25. On this theme of the private law consequences of prohibited acts see also Warren, supra, note 15; Goodhart, supra, note 15.
26. The judge recognised arguments made by counsel for the bank (which is examined further in the text below) that administrative acts designated as "void" or "invalid" may have legal effect in view of the court's discretion in judicial review proceedings to decline a remedy to invalidate such acts. However, he determined that since the court has no such discretion in private law actions, the absence of capacity required that the act be treated as without legal effect in such proceedings.
27. Warren, supra, note 14, at p.191.
28. (1612) 77 E.R. 937.
29. In some cases it may be merely a particular undertaking in a contract which is unlawful and not the subject matter of the contract as a whole as, for example, in *Roberts v Hopwood* [1925] A.C. 578 where the House of Lords held that local authorities could not pay employees greater than market rates under the legislation applicable at that time. The approach to unlawful terms should be the same as to unlawful subject matter. Thus, if contracts for an unlawful subject matter are generally unenforceable against the authority, a particular unlawful undertaking should likewise be unenforceable. This will, however, raise the difficult question of how far such unenforceable terms might be severed from the contract as a whole. On the way in which the courts have dealt with these issues in the context of "illegal" contracts see G.H. Treitel, *The Law of Contract* (9th ed. 1995; London, Sweet & Maxwell, pp.459-65.
30. See Treitel, supra, ch.11 esp. pp.438-66.
31. *James v Commonwealth* (1939) 62 C.L.R. 339.

32.   *Ormiston v Great Western Railway* [1917] 1 K.B. 598 at 602 per Rowlatt J; and see Warren and Goodhart, supra, note 14.

33.   Cane, supra, note 14, p.517.

34.   Arrowsmith, Warren and Cane, supra, note 14.

35.   This should require knowledge of the facts, where relevant (for example, where the legality of the transaction depends on the motive of the authority - for example, the purpose of a loan), and also of the relevant public law (although ignorance of the criminal law does render a party "innocent" in the case of contracts made in contravention of the criminal law).

36.   Companies Act 1985, s.35(1), as am. by Companies Act 1989, s.108, and Companies Act 1989, s.108, as inserted by Companies Act 1989, s.109.

37.   Local Government Act 1972, sch.13, para. 10.

38.   Even before the recent liberalisation of standing rules this was recognised as one of the interests giving standing to challenge a decision in public law.

39.   This follows from the House of Lords decision in *Roy v Kensington and Chelsea and Westminster Family Practitioner Committee* [1992] 1 A.C. 624.

40.   S.I. 1991 no. 2680.

41.   S.I. 1993 no. 3228.

42.   S.I. 1995 no. 201.

43.   S.I. 1993 no. 3228.

44.   Directive 93/37/EEC, (1993) O.J. L 199/54 (on public works contracts); directive 92/50/EEC, (1993) O.J. L 209/1 (on public services contracts); directive 93/36/EEC, (1993) O.J. L 199/1; (public supply contracts); directive 89/685/EEC, (1989) O.J. L 395/33 (on remedies for enforcing the public sector rules); directive 93/38/EEC, (1993) O.J. L 199/84 (on utilities contracts); directive 92/13/EEC, (1992) O.J. L/76/7 (on remedies for enforcing the utilities rules).

45.   [1988] 1 All E.R. 938.

46.   These points even apply where the rule is concerned with the choice of whether to enter into a particular transaction at all: even if the transaction would not have been made if the safeguard had been followed, this may be considered less serious than breach of an absolute restriction on certain transactions, and there is still the possibility that the transaction would have gone ahead anyway.

47.   *Young v Royal Leamington* [1883] 8 A.C. 517; *Rhyl UDC v Rhyl Amusements* [1959] 1 W.L.R. 465; *Mellis v Shirley Local Board* (1885) 16 Q.B.D.446; *Lawford v Billericay R.D.C.* [1903]1 K.B.772.

48.   See, in particular, the decision of the High Court of Australia in *Australian Broadcasting Corp. v Redmore* (1989) 166 C.L.R. 454 (in which the authority sought to evade the contract). On the Canadian

decisions see S. Arrowsmith, *Government Procurement and Judicial Review* (1988) ch.14.

49. In most cases the question of specific performance will not arise but if it does the court should balance the public and private interests involved.

50. The relevant provisions, set out in Order 53, r.4 and Supreme Court Act 1988, s.31(6), are not entirely clear, but were interpreted in the manner set out in the text in the House of Lords decision in *R. v Dairy Produce Quota Tribunal, ex parte Caswell* [1990] 2 A.C.738.

51. The court may hold that an application is not prompt even if made within three months, and is likely to do so in procurement cases in view of the need for prompt action to avoid disrupting government programmes.

52. Ibid.

53. For the cases see Bingham, "Should Public Law Remedies be Discretionary?" [1991] P.L.64.

54. C.f. however, Environmental Protection Act 1990, 5.51 and Sch.2.Pt II, para 2a(1), stating that contracts awarded in breach of tendering provisions for local authority waste disposal contracts are void. This can be explained on the basis that the provisions are aimed mainly at preventing favouritism towards companies controlled by the local authority itself, although wholly independent third parties could be affected.

55. Public Works Contracts Regulations, supra, reg.31(7); Public Supply Contracts Regulations, supra, reg. 29(6); Public Services Contracts Regulations, supra, reg. 32(6); Utilities Contracts Regulations, supra.

56. On this point see further the discussion under the heading "Challenges to the contract by way of judicial review". In addition, a contract may possibly be required to be set aside by the government, by legislation if necessary, following a declaration by the Court of Justice that the contract is contrary to Community law, pursuant to Article 177 EC (which requires states to take the measures necessary to comply with a decision of the Court). That the set aside of a contract may be required here may be deduced from the fact that the court has the power to award interim measures to suspend a concluded contract: see case C-272/91R, *Commission v Italy*, orders of 31 January 1992 and 12 June 1992 ("Lottomatica") and case C-87/94R, *Commission v Belgium,* order of 22 April 1994. However, it can be argued that such measures against concluded contracts are only possible where national law itself allows for a contract to be set aside which in the United Kingdom would, as explained below, apply (if at all) only where the other party knows of the breach.

57. See *R v Hereford Corporation ex parte Harrower* [1970] 1 W.L.R. 1424 (on the Local Government Act).

58. Directive 89/665/EEC, supra, Article 2(6) and Directive 92/13/EEC, supra, Article 2(6).

59. Limitations on effective remedies may be maintained to protect "legitimate interests" of third parties affected by state action, but a party may not be considered to have such a legitimate interest where he knows or should have known of the breach of Community law: see case 5/89, *Commission v Germany* [1990] I-E.C.R. 3437, concerned with recovery of unlawful state aids. The case concerned centralised enforcement proceedings, not an action in the national courts, but the Court of Justice made it clear that the same principles apply in both cases.

60. *Burroughes v Oxford Area Health Authority*, July 21, 1983 (unreported; transcript on Lexis).

61. See J.D.B. Mitchell, *The Contracts of Public Authorities* (1954); I.Rogerson, "On the Fettering of Public Powers" [1971] P.L. 288; S. Arrowsmith, *Civil Liability and Public Authorities* (1992), pp.72-9; P.P.Craig, *Administrative Law* (3rd ed. 1994), pp.699-707.

62. See Craig, supra, p.709; Arrowsmith, supra, pp.125-6; P.W. Hogg, *Liability of the Crown* (1989), p.175.

63. *Western Fish Products v Penrith D.C.* [1981] 2 All E.R. 204. See Craig, supra, ch.18.

64. *Ridge v Baldwin* [1964] A.C. 40; *Malloch v Aberdeen Corporation* [1971] 1 W.L.R. 1578. For further discussion of this point see S. Arrowsmith, *Civil Liability and Public Authorities* (1992), pp.90-2 and pp.134-6.

2   The "Europeanisation" of Contract Law

HUGH BEALE

In some ways, contract law seems an unlikely candidate for "Europeanisation". Much of contract law is concerned with filling any gaps in what the parties have agreed. In principle, the parties can establish their own rules to govern their relationship and the starting point of most if not all the laws of contract of EU Member States is that, within the confines set by doctrines of illegality and immorality, *pacta sunt servanda*; what has been agreed will be enforced.

However there can be no doubt that differences between national laws do add barriers to trade between Member States. To discover your rights in another Member State, or to ensure that a contract provision will have the same effect as in your own State, can be a time-consuming and therefore expensive business.[1] Needless to say, set against a multi-million ECU contract, this cost may be slight; but in other situations, particularly small purchases by consumers or businesses, the uncertainty and the cost of remedying it can lead to a form of market failure in which the transaction cost prevents what would otherwise be wealth-maximising exchanges taking place.

Thus it is not surprising to find that there are moves to create a "European" law of contract. There are other motives also. One is to eliminate competitive advantages derived from differing legal systems and thus to level the playing field for firms from different Member States to compete on a more equal footing. Another, perhaps less publicly articulated but probably quite strong among the workers involved in the various projects, is to establish bonds between the various States by emphasising what their legal systems have in common. Many lawyers, especially on the Continent, originally aimed at harmonisation or unification even of the private law of Member States. Thus in 1989 the European Parliament passed a Resolution requesting a start on work on a European Code of Private Law. The preamble to the Resolution states:

... unification can be carried out in branches of private law which are highly important for the development of a single Market, such as contract law.[2]

Since the Maastricht Treaty and the adoption of the principle of subsidiarity, actual unification seems less likely. Whether subsidiarity is seen as a legal principle delimiting the competence of the European authorities, a political principle or merely a description of the political process,[3] it reflects what is probably still the predominant view that intervention by Brussels should be limited to what is necessary. It is very doubtful whether a convincing argument could be made for compelling all Member States to adopt the same private law. Nor would it necessarily be desirable. I share Hugh Collins' view that there is a value in preserving the cultural diversity which our differing laws represent.[4] Just where the line is between preserving these differences and eliminating barriers to economic integration is a matter for debate.[5]

Nonetheless, "Europeanisation" of contract law at a lower level than proposed unification is proceeding apace. Firstly, it is being created directly through the various Directives which impinge on contract. These are primarily in the consumer field.[6] Second, it is being "discovered" by the creation of international restatements which attempt to weld together the common features and principles of the various laws of contract into a harmonious and workable whole. In fact the only complete restatement[7] so far published is international rather than European: the UNIDROIT *Principles of International Commercial Contracts*.[8] But the Commission on European Contract Law[9] has just published Part I of a European equivalent: *The Principles of European Contract Law, Part I*, which deals with "Performance, Non-performance and Remedies" (PECL).

Although the Commission on European Contract Law expresses the hope that the Principles may be used as a model for any future harmonisation,[10] the Principles have more immediate aims. They can be applied by arbitrators when the parties have opted for arbitration according to "general principles of contract law", "internationally accepted principles" and the like.[11] In international contracts such clauses are not uncommon as neither party may wish to subject the contract to the law of the other party's state.[12] Or the parties may expressly incorporate the Principles into their agreement.[13]

At a less direct level, the Commission hopes that the Principles will help to establish an agreed terminology and set of concepts for future European legislation,[14] and will be a source of inspiration for legislators and judges developing the national laws of Member States, present and aspiring.[15]

Such restatements do not pose any direct threat to national laws. Nor is this kind of work incompatible with subsidiarity - indeed the reverse. Neither the provision of rules for application to international contracts nor the establishment of a terminology or agreed concepts is something which Member States can do effectively on their own. Perhaps the European Parliament's repetition on 6 May 1994 of its earlier resolution, and the continued financial support for the work from the European Commission and elsewhere, reflect this.

In the first part of this Chapter I will argue that "Europeanisation" of contract law in the two ways I have mentioned looks set to continue; in particular, I anticipate increasing intervention both in and outside the field of consumer contracts. But if direct intervention through legislation from Brussels does extend to more aspects of commercial contracts, the work will become more difficult. Some of this will be technical difficulty caused by the different concepts used in the various laws and the sheer complexity of the subject. Some will be caused by apparently divergent aims and contrasting philosophies which will have to be reconciled if measures are to have any chance of success. I will illustrate some of the difficulties by looking in the second part of the Chapter at efforts in the area of what may be called "misapprehensions" - broadly speaking, what in English law is treated under the rubrics of mistake and misrepresentation.

European Directives

Some Directives which we may think of as affecting general contract law[16] already apply to commercial contracts; notably the Directive on Self-employed Commercial Agents[17] and the various Directives governing the letting of many forms of public contract. These include contracts for public services, supply and works; public procurement in water, energy, transport and communications services; and public procurement of construction products.[18] The public procurement Directives are aimed at strengthening the Single Market by encouraging competition and preventing discrimination against firms from other Member States. This is to be achieved by increasing the transparency of tendering and award procedures and giving aggrieved tenderers a remedy if the proper procedures are not used.

Consumer protection Directives

The majority, however, have been concerned with the protection of consumers. Whereas the earlier Directives such as that on Liability for Defective Products[19] were justified primarily in terms of "levelling the playing field", the emphasis now seems as much on completion of the Single Market by increasing the consumer's confidence to buy abroad. Thus the Preamble to the Directive on Unfair Terms in Consumer Contracts refers both to distortion of competition arising from differing legal regimes[20] and to consumer confidence:

Whereas, generally speaking, consumers do not know the rules of law which, in Member States other than their own, govern contracts for the sale of goods and services; whereas this lack of awareness may deter them from direct transactions for the purchase of goods or services in another Member State;...[21]

Removal of these differences, it is argued, will facilitate the establishment of the internal market by helping sellers and suppliers to sell or supply and thereby increase competition.[22]

Meanwhile, as a result of the Maastricht Treaty consumer protection is now directly within the competence of the Community[23] and is seen as an end itself.[24]

The impact of Directives on general contract law (including for this purpose consumer contracts in general) adopted to date is of course significant, particularly the Directive on Unfair Terms. The "Doorstep sales" Directive[25] and those regulating consumer credit[26] had been largely anticipated in the UK by Consumer Credit Act 1974; and even the Product Liability Directive had been largely foreshadowed by previous proposals.[27] Neither was true of the Unfair Terms Directive.

This Directive has been discussed in detail elsewhere.[28] For present purposes it will suffice to note that, although the Regulations implementing the Directive enable the courts to strike down a much greater range of unfair clauses than is possible under Unfair Contract Terms Act 1977 and other UK legislation, the private law technique employed seems broadly familiar.[29] The test of whether a term is unfair is cast in unfamiliar language: a term is unfair

> ... if, contrary to the requirement of good faith, it causes a significant imbalance in the parties' rights and obligations arising under the contract, to the detriment of the consumer.[30]

The possibility that "fairness" under this test and "reasonableness" under UCTA may differ was one reason why the Department of Trade and Industry chose separate implementation of the Directive by regulations.[31] But it seems that under the German Act on Standard Contract Terms of 1976,[32] from which the Directive test appears to be derived, the courts apply the test in a similar way to reasonableness.[33]

Collins has justly remarked that in terms of ensuring a minimal guaranteed protection for consumers, the Directive on Unfair Terms does little: its restriction to terms "which have not been individually negotiated"[34] was a victory for those who wanted to deal simply with market failures due to consumer ignorance as to what they were "agreeing", and perhaps lack of choice.[35] But curiously this limitation may in the long run lead to a wider control of contracts in general than if the Directive had included the Article, at one stage proposed, which would make a term, whether or not individually negotiated, unfair if it

> caused the performance of the contract to be unduly detrimental to the

consumer.[36]

This is because, even if such a provision might have been accepted in relation to consumer contracts, I cannot see that it would ever be so in relation to commercial contracts. Yet I think there may be pressure in the future to extend the Directive in its present "market failure" approach in the direction of commercial contracts.

Consumer guarantees

This pressure may come if the Council adopts a new Directive on "guarantees" in sale of goods. In 1993 the European Commission circulated a *Green Paper on Guarantees for Consumer Goods and After-sales Services*.[37] To an English lawyer the use of the word "guarantee" in this context may seem odd. It is used in the continental sense to refer to the responsibility of the seller (and in some systems, the manufacturer and others in the distribution chain) for the goods being free from defects (referred to as the "legal guarantee") as well as to the kind of guarantee voluntarily offered by manufacturers, importers and sometimes retailers themselves (the "commercial guarantee").

Again the paper stresses the importance of consumer confidence:

> ... appropriate guarantees and after-sales service conditions are important if consumers are to be encouraged to benefit from the opportunities offered by the Single Market. Cross-border shopping can only flourish if the consumer knows he will enjoy the same guarantee and after-sales service conditions no matter where the supplier is located.[38]

> The large economic space without frontiers will not be completely realised unless, in conjunction with the free movement of products and services, the "free movement" of consumers can be secured as purchasers of goods and recipients of services...

> Strengthening the confidence of consumers in the large market and encouraging consumers to take an active part in its functioning means that conditions must be created so that the consumers can rest assured as to their rights and know they can definitely rely on them throughout the single market.[39]

At one time drafts of the Directive on Unfair Terms contained proposals on this subject. Thus in 1992 the Commission submitted to the Council an amended proposal[40] which included the following:

Article 6

1. The Member States shall take the necessary measures in order to ensure that the consumer is guaranteed, as purchaser under a contract for the sale of goods, the right to receive goods which are in conformity with the

contract and are fit for the purpose for which they were sold, and to complain, within an appropriately extensive period, about any intrinsic defects which the goods may contain.

2. For the purposes of exercising these rights, the Member States shall take the necessary measures in order to ensure that the consumer is guaranteed the choice of the following available options:
- the reimbursement of the whole of the purchase price,
- the replacement of the goods,
- the repair of the goods at the seller's expense,
- a reduction in the price if the consumer retains the goods,

and the right to compensation for damage sustained by him which arises out of the contract.

3. In cases in which the seller transmits to the consumer the guarantee of the manufacturer of the goods, the Member States shall take the necessary measures in order to ensure that the consumer is guaranteed the right to benefit from the manufacturer's guarantee for a period of 12 months or for the normal working life of the goods, where this is less than 12 months, and to enforce payment, either by the seller or by the manufacturer, of the costs incurred by the consumer in obtaining implementation of that guarantee.

4. The Member States shall take the necessary measures to ensure that the consumer is guaranteed, as purchaser under a contract for the supply of services, the right:
- to be supplied with those services at the agreed time and with all due efficiency,
- to have the supplier's warranty that the supplier has the requisite skill and expertise to supply the services in the manner specified in the foregoing indent.

The Council decided that this draft Article should be withdrawn but invited the Commission to examine the matter and, if appropriate, submit a separate proposal on the matter. The Green Paper is the outcome in relation to sales.[41]

This is not the place for a detailed consideration of the Green paper, particularly as

...the Commission does not claim to present either pat solutions or even to come out in favour of one or the other at this stage... The Green Paper simply presents a number of options which seem appropriate.[42]

The suggestions on after-sales services are extremely sketchy and in fact relate only to the provision of spare parts.[43] Those on the "commercial" guarantee are also obviously at an early stage.[44] Beyond a suggestion that if a commercial guarantee is given it should be legally enforceable,[45] little work had been done on how to reconcile the Commission's evident desire to ensure that commercial guarantees have some minimum content, and in particular offer the consumer something beyond the legal guarantee, with the notion that the commercial guarantee is voluntary.

On the legal guarantee the solutions canvassed are broadly in line with the earlier draft, though the more detailed analysis given in the Green paper shows that the bland words of the earlier draft may contain surprises to the English lawyer. Thus the Green paper makes it clear that it is envisaged that manufacturers as well as retailers would be directly liable to the consumer. This is thought to be important for cross-border shopping:

> ...it is very difficult for a consumer to return to a foreign vendor in order to complain about a product defect. Normally it will be a lot easier for him to address a representative or a branch of the manufacturer in his own country.[46]

This simple statement seems to beg a number of major questions about the legal responsibility, or even the commercial attitude, of representatives of a manufacturer in one state in relation to the manufacturer's goods which were sold in another State; but the basic argument for making manufacturers responsible seems sound.[47] Manufacturers are already responsible in Belgium, France and Luxembourg, but it would be a radical change for the law of some other Member States, e.g. German law and of course English law - though the Commission seems to have been encouraged by the provisional proposals along similar lines made by the Department of Trade and Industry.[48]

The consultation on the Green Paper produced a reasonably favourable response. It was reported to a European Consumer Forum in October 1994[49] that a majority of the replies had been generally favourable. The Council invited the Commission to submit its conclusions[50] and the Commissioner responsible for consumer affairs has announced that a draft Directive will be prepared.[51]

Extension to commercial contracts?

What is of particular interest for the purpose of this paper is the scope the new Directive might have. The Unfair Terms Directive is limited to "consumers", defined as

> any natural persons who, in contracts covered by this Directive, is acting for purposes which are outside his trade, business or profession.[52]

Thus a company cannot claim the protection of the Directive.[53] But the Green Paper envisages defining consumer not in relation to the "subjective" status of the purchaser of goods but "objectively" in relation to the goods themselves. Thus if a company were to buy a car, a personal computer or anything else not uncommonly sold to consumers, it might be within the scope of the Directive.

This broader scope cannot easily be justified in terms of consumer protection, but it can be in terms of completing the single market. The new proposals are largely addressed at problems of market failure. In all of these cases, the relevant reason the consumer or other buyer may be deterred from "shopping abroad" is that it is very costly either to find out what rights she will have under the foreign legal system,[54] or to negotiate better ones. These transactions costs apply just as much to occasional purchases by business buyers as they do to purchases by individual consumers.

This raises a more fundamental point. Why should we stop at goods ordinarily supplied to consumers? Surely we wish to encourage "cross-border" shopping by businesses just as much as by consumers. It is no doubt easier to get consensus among Member States for action to protect consumers, since most already have their own schemes of consumer protection; but the problems are just the same and the potential gains from removing barriers are just as large. These points were made by Collins in relation to unfair terms but they apply also to legal guarantees.[55]

Whether the Commission's proposal will move in this direction, even to the extent of protecting businesses which buy "consumer" goods, remains to be seen. There is in the Green Paper still the tension between aims of "merely" correcting market failure and of giving consumers minimum guaranteed rights.[56] But if, as with the Directive on Unfair Terms, the "free marketeers" concerned with correcting failures win the day, that seems to make extension of the proposals to protect businesses easier. Nor should this seem extreme. In the United Kingdom, the Unfair Contract Terms Act 1977 protects even businesses from unreasonable limitation of liability and exclusion clauses in standard form contracts[57] and, in relation to the description and quality of goods, supply of goods contracts.[58]

It is true that, if the provisions of any Directive on legal guarantees were extended to apply to business purchases generally, its scope might be wider than necessary. When a business is making a particular type of purchase regularly, e.g. buying parts from other manufacturers, it is likely to acquire a fair degree of expertise and the relative cost of negotiating a suitable contract with its supplier is much lower. It does not need to "have its hand held". However this over-inclusiveness need not be of concern for two reasons.

Firstly, it will always be open to the business and its supplier to modify their rights and obligations by express agreement. So far as present European law is concerned, this freedom is unrestricted, as the Directive on Unfair Terms will not apply. It would be sensible to match any Directive on legal guarantees by an extension of the Directive on Unfair Terms; it would make little sense to lay down an elaborate scheme of legal guarantees for contracts made by businesses if its provisions could simply be negated by the supplier's general conditions. But even then suppliers would have little to fear from European law. The Unfair Terms Directive does not even create a presumption that any term is unfair.[59] Thus the control is significantly weaker than that already imposed on such exclusion clauses in United Kingdom law.

Secondly, the content of the proposals made in the Green Paper is actually quite mild. In English law we are accustomed to think in terms of contractual liability being "full" liability - i.e. to include compensation for what are popularly called "consequential losses".[60] In relation to a consumer sale, this is not so burdensome: once questions of personal injury and property damage are put on one side,[61] most consumers are concerned with getting the goods repaired or replaced or their money back. Consequential economic losses beyond, perhaps, the cost of hiring a substitute while repairs are being done are likely to be minimal. With businesses, however, the picture is very different. The failure of a computer at a critical moment can cause extensive economic loss. Immediate sellers and certainly manufacturers are likely to be reluctant to accept responsibility for economic loss of this kind because its extent is unpredictable to the seller and therefore expensive to insure on a liability basis.[62]

The continental model of the "legal guarantee" is somewhat less demanding. The seller or manufacturer is primarily liable to refund the price or pay the amount by which the item is worth less by reason of the defect. In fact in many systems this is in practice no longer the position for most cases; for example French law imposes liability for damages if the vendor knew of the defect, and in the case of a professional seller knowledge is presumed irrebuttably.[63] Although the draft article considered by the Council and withdrawn in 1992[64] would have made suppliers responsible for "damage... which arises out of the contract", the Green Paper suggests basing the Directive more on the traditional model. The seller's or manufacturer's responsibility would be to repair the product, to replace it with one in working order, to refund part of the price or to take back the product and refund the price. The question of compensation in damages would be left to Member States.[65]

This provision would be significantly less burdensome than the earlier draft. I rather doubt whether sellers would wish to exclude even a business buyer from these rights, though it might want to be able to choose which to give rather than to have to allow the buyer to choose as the Green paper contemplates.

Thus I anticipate that there will be pressure, at least, to extend direct intervention from Brussels from merely consumer sales to at least some business sales. The rationale which seems to underlie both the Unfair Terms Directive and the proposals on legal guarantees applies just as much to business sales. Here too a form of market failure caused by the cost of discovering the law of other Member States, or of negotiating terms, is likely to hinder the development of the Single Market.

Some of the difficulties of "Europeanisation"

I hope I have also said enough to show some of the difficulties which are caused by trying to legislate for a variety of legal systems. Terms such as "legal guarantee" are unfamiliar to common lawyers; the automatic assumption of common lawyers that "responsibility" for defects means full responsibility for even consequential loss is alien to many civil lawyers. It is difficulties of this kind which I wish to illustrate in more detail in the second part of this Chapter.

"Misapprehensions" in contract

The scope of the existing and proposed Directives affecting general contract law is, as suggested at the start of the paper, fairly limited. The field of operation is readily identified and most of the techniques employed, though at first in a strange terminology, turn out to be broadly familiar to English lawyers - or at least fairly easy to grasp. When we turn to the international restatements, however, problems of differing concepts and differing uses of terminology become much more difficult. Moreover, as suggested earlier, there seems to be much less agreement on the underlying aims and values of the law.

In fact these problems do not just occur in the course of developing restatements. Few areas of contract law are wholly self-contained; so that even a Directive on a particular topic may need to refer to concepts which are broader than the topic or to concepts which are in "another part" of contract law. "Good faith" in the Unfair Terms Directive is an example of the former. The reference in the draft Unfair Terms Directive quoted earlier to the seller's responsibility for damages is an example of the latter. When considering whether specific provisions are needed on the extent of the seller's liability, it would be helpful to have a "model" of what liability for damages in contract looks like across Europe. The Principles of European Contract Law Part I, provide such a model.[66] The Principles are accompanied by notes comparing the rules stated by the Principles to the various national laws.

Misapprehensions in contract

However, to illustrate the more general thesis, this Section explores an area of law not unrelated to the problem of the legal guarantee: the question of the party who has entered a contract under some kind of misapprehension as to what she was getting, or the value of her own performance. This is a topic on which the Commission on European Contract Law is currently working.[67]

The technical difficulties of the area arise principally from the number of different rules bearing on the subject. Indeed, so many concepts are used that it is not always easy to identify the subject the problem the law is seeking to solve.[68] For present purposes I will define it thus: what relief, if any, should be given when one party or each of them has entered a contract under some misapprehension about what it is that she has contracted to give or do, or has

32

contracted to receive. Misapprehension must be taken broadly to include the case where a party knows what item she is to convey or receive but is not aware of all of its characteristics. For the sake of space I arbitrarily exclude the case where the misapprehension relates to the identity or attributes of the other party. I use the word "misapprehension" in an attempt to find a neutral term which does not have legal overtones carried by, for example, "mistake", since we shall see that the overtones may be very different for the different legal systems.

The English rules

There is a multiplicity of doctrines even in the English law on this topic. First, there is an overlap between "misapprehensions" and the legal guarantee, or as English lawyers would more usually put it, the implied terms of the contract. In many cases which we think of as falling under what was discussed in Section 1, the buyer, and probably also the seller, wrongly assumed that the goods to be supplied were in accordance with the contract and free from defects when they were not. This is by so far the most common case that it is doubtful whether there will ever be a call for European Directives going beyond it. International restatements, however, have to deal with the broader problem.

In English law it would also be relevant to ask whether any express undertakings or "warranties" had been given by either party to the other;[69] and, even if no undertakings were given, whether there had been any misrepresentation of fact by one party to the other. If there has been a misstatement of fact which the other has relied on, English law readily gives a remedy. First, the misrepresentee may rescind the contract. Originally this remedy was available as of right even in cases of fairly unimportant misrepresentations.[70] Since 1967 the court has had discretion, in cases where there was no fraud, to refuse rescission and award damages in lieu of rescission if this seems more equitable.[71] Damages may be recovered as of right if the misrepresentation was fraudulent or if the misrepresentor is unable to prove that he believed, and had reasonable grounds to believe, that what he said was true.[72]

Lastly, an English lawyer might consider the doctrine of mistake. There might be a mistake over the terms,[73] which is probably best viewed as an aspect of formation; or a mistake about the subject matter. The latter is relevant only if the mistake is fundamental and if it was common to the two parties.[74] In practice so many of the cases are dealt with under the doctrines of express or implied terms or of misrepresentation that mistake cases are very rare.

Common ground with French and German law

Space permits only a brief comparison of English law to two continental systems, those of France and Germany. There is obviously some common ground between the three systems. First, the English implied terms are matched by the continental legal guarantee. Even here there are significant differences. For example, the implied terms under the English Sale of Goods Act 1979, that the goods will be of satisfactory quality[75] and fit for any particular purpose that the buyer has made known to the seller,[76] apply only to sales made in the course of a business; and there is normally no warranty against hidden physical defects in the case of land. French law does not limit its *garantie de vice caché* to business sales nor to goods.[77] On the other hand, under English law the seller's responsibility is full, whereas we saw earlier that under French law the non-professional seller is only liable for damages if he knew of the defect.

There are also apparently close parallels between the systems in relation to fraud, though as we shall see, continental systems have a wider notion of what types of conduct can constitute fraud. However, they often require an intention to deceive, whereas in English law a statement is fraudulent if it was known to be false even if it was made without any intention to cause loss.[78]

Misrepresentation and self-induced mistake

Once we move away from these two topics, however, the differences become more apparent. Perhaps the most striking is this. English law draws a sharp distinction between cases in which one party misleads the other and cases of "self-deception". In cases where misleading information has been given, it is very ready to give relief. Thus a misrepresentee may rescind the contract, or at least recover damages in lieu of rescission, for any material untrue statement, even if the other party made the statement honestly and without negligence. There will be liability in damages on a tortious basis if the misrepresentor was at fault; and if the statement was important[79] and it was reasonable to rely on what the other party said, the statement is likely to be treated as a contractual promise.[80] The approach of French and German law to such problems is in marked contrast. An express guarantee by the seller is possible but it appears that a much clearer expression of intention is required than in English law.[81] Outside cases of fraud, most of the burden seems to be carried by the doctrine of mistake. In neither system is this limited to cases of common mistake, and relief is frequently given under this heading when in English law the case would be dealt with as misrepresentation.

Mistake caused by the other party in French and German law

In principle, in either system relief will be given only for mistakes which are serious. In French law, the mistake must relate to the substance of the subject matter.[82] Errors of motive do not give rise to relief.[83] Thus if a person buys land with the plan of building a filling station to serve what she had wrongly assumed would remain a main road, she will not get relief. This is clearly stricter than the minimal requirement of English law that the misrepresentation

34

be material.

However, the jurisprudence has interpreted "substance" broadly. Relief may be given where the mistake related to some matter which was a "determining consideration",[84] or some quality without which it is clear that a buyer would not have bought; e.g. where the area of land purchased was smaller than he supposed and inadequate for the building scheme he intended.[85] It is not sufficient that the quality was essential as far as the buyer was concerned: it must also have been evident to the seller that this was the case, though following the jurisprudence the essential quality need not have been part of the agreement (*convenu*).[86] But it is clear that the requirements for mistake are much less severe than the "essentially different" test used in the English doctrine of common mistake.[87]

Under German law a contract may be set aside on the ground of error as to the quality of the subject-matter if the quality was determining for the mistaken party and was essential.[88] Relief is not given for errors of motive[89] but essential qualities may include any characteristic of the subject matter, e.g. the age of a car sold.[90] The test is whether the person would have made the declaration he did had he known and reasonably understood the situation. This seems less demanding than the test in French law. It has been said, however, that the mistake must be as to something which would influence a reasonable person.[91] And if the German doctrine of mistake seems more liberal than the French, it must be noted that it has a unique way of protecting the interests of the other party. Under BGB §122, the party against whom relief is sought is entitled to damages calculated on the reliance interest basis,[92] unless he knew or should have known of the mistake.[93]

Under both systems, as well as avoiding the contract the disappointed party may be able to claim damages from the other party if the latter was at fault, on the basis of general delictual responsibility in French law[94] or *culpa in contrahendo* in German law.[95]

Perhaps because it concentrates on the behaviour of the misrepresentor in seeking to hold the other to a contract which he obtained by giving incorrect information, the English doctrine of misrepresentation is in one way more generous than the French doctrine of mistake. English law allows rescission even though the misrepresentee could have discovered the truth for himself, whereas under the French doctrine mistake must not be inexcusable. In German law, however, fault on the part of the mistaken party is irrelevant.[96]

Thus both French and German law regularly allow avoidance of the contract when one party has misled the other and so in English law the case would be dealt with as one of misrepresentation.[97] The techniques are different but the results by and large similar. Just what practical differences there are between the various tests - "substance of the subject matter", "determining quality of the subject matter", "material" misrepresentation - is much harder to gauge without a detailed examination of the decisions in each jurisdiction, which cannot be undertaken here.

If we move away from mistakes caused by incorrect information, much greater differences between the systems become apparent. Two illustrations will make this clear.

The first is the case where the party's misapprehension is about the terms to which she has agreed: to take the simplest case, the situation where she has made a slip of the pen and has written, say, £1,000 when she meant to write £1,200. In English law the rule appears quite strict: the other party can take what was written at face value unless he knows that it was not what the first party meant. It is not even clear that the mistaken party can get relief if the other party should have known that there had been a mistake: the rectification cases suggest that only actual knowledge, or a suspicion of a mistake coupled with sharp practice, will suffice.[98]

In French law the matter is complicated. On occasion the courts apply the theory that an *erreur obstacle* may prevent a sufficient meeting of the minds for a contract to come into existence; at other times they seem to stretch the theory of error as to the substance in order to deal with such cases.[99] But it is clearly not a requirement that the mistake be known to the other party.

In German law, error in declaration was originally the only case covered by BGB §119, the provision on error as to the substance being added only later. Thus relief will be given if someone bids for a car at an auction thinking mistakenly that he is bidding for a quite different vehicle; or if he types the wrong price in his offer.[100] The same applies if the mistake is made by an agency charged with transmitting the message.[101] In the example given where a party writes £1,000 when she means £1,200, German law would begin by asking whether the other party was in fact misled by the slip. If in fact he knew that she meant £1,200, there will be a meeting of minds and a valid contract at £1,200: *falsa demonstratio non nocet*. But if even he did not know, then relief seems possible under BGB§119(1). The writer's mind did not go with her act.

Thus the contrast with English law is remarkable. It is true that the German rule is tempered by the provision for damages described earlier; French law therefore seems the most liberal - and therefore to give the non-mistaken party the least security.

Self-induced mistake and duties of disclosure in French and German law

The difference in approach has its most dramatic outcome in the second illustration, cases of self-induced misapprehensions as to substance, as opposed to the terms of the contract. Unless the case is one that falls under the implied terms of the relevant type of contract, English law normally gives a remedy only in cases in which both parties have made the same mistake. This is not true of either French or German law.[102] And while the importance of the matter must be apparent to the other party, the latter need not know or even have reason to know that the mistake has occurred.

Further, a party who knows or ought to know that the other is or may be labouring under a mistake may have an obligation to correct any misapprehension. The developments in French law have been described in detail by other writers,[103] and a brief note will have to suffice here. Provided the non-mistaken party intended the other to be deceived, he may be guilty of *dol par réticence*: in contrast to the requirement for fraud in English law for a representation by words or conduct, in French law mere silence can amount to *dol*. The courts have also imposed a duty on some (usually but not exclusively professional) parties to disclose information which is known to be critical to the other party and of which the other was excusably ignorant. There must also be legitimate reliance by the other party on the first party. The duty may be broken without any intention to deceive, though in the absence of *dol* the only remedy will be damages.

In German law too, keeping silent when there is a duty to speak may amount to fraud under BGB §123(1).[104] This is based on good faith and whether there will be a duty to disclose depends upon the degree of confidence between the parties and the nature of the contract. But there may be duty to disclose in sales cases: e.g. the seller of a used car was held to be under a duty to tell the buyer that the car had been in a serious accident which had caused permanent damage to the chassis[105] and an estate agent to disclose his suspicion that a house suffers from rot.[106]

Thus in these systems a party may be able to avoid the contract on the ground of a misapprehension which the other party did not even know about, let alone cause or share. And where the other party knew or should have known of the relevant information, he may now also be under a duty to disclose the information. Failure to do so may lead to avoidance of the contract or make him liable in damages.

Reasons for the divergences in approach

These differences seem to be the result of the well-known differences in approach between the common law and the civil law. The common law has traditionally stressed the reasonable appearance of consent to the other party, and tends to allow relief only if the latter has in some way acted badly, each by not pointing out a known error. The civil law traditionally places much more emphasis on the will of the mistaken party.[107] But the fact that the systems had differences originally does not fully explain why these differences have persisted. Is there some other reason for the continued divergence?

One possibility is that the legal systems reflect differing societal values - for example, English law ranking security of transactions more highly than French or German law or the continental systems taking a more "moral" view.[108] Collins has made the point that cultural values are deeply imbedded in the law of each country, which in turn helps shape cultural identity. He suggests that over time a new "European" identity may emerge, but that until then there may be considerable difficulties in the way of harmonising the national solutions.[109] I accept completely the general thrust of Collins' argument. There are some problems - his example of the trade in human organs is a good one - where cultural attitudes even within Western Europe may differ so much that at present it would be very difficult to agree on a common solution. This is one reason why neither UNIDROIT nor the draft PECL rules on validity deal with immorality or illegality. What I am not sure is that the problem of non-disclosure falls into this category. Discussions within the Commission on European Contract Law do not suggest this so much as that whether disclosure should be required should vary from case to case.

My own view is that the divergences on this point reflect the differing cases which are presented to each legal system for its decision.[110] Open any text on English contract and it is immediately clear that our common law is driven by commercial cases where the whole aim of the system is to beat the other party at his own game. Results such as that in the notorious *Poussin* case - in which a buyer for the Louvre spotted that a painting sold as by an artist of the school of Carracci might well be by Poussin and bought it at a relatively low price; the Louvre was forced to return the painting when it was attributed to the more famous artist[111] - actually seem wrong to English lawyers. If I have developed an expertise in spotting lost masterpieces, surely I should be allowed to make use of it, just as a commercial buyer should be able to take advantage of her better knowledge of the market?[112]

The approach of the restatements

In a "restatement" of the principles of contract law in Europe or internationally, how are these difficulties to be reconciled? Just as the Restatement in the United States had frequently to adopt what seemed the better rule, so too the Principles. Not surprisingly, both the UNIDROIT text and the current draft of the Principles of European Contract Law (PECL) take a via media. Thus the current draft of PECL contains the following article on mistake:

Mistake as to facts or law[113]
(1) A party may avoid a contract for mistake of fact or law existing when the contract was concluded if
(a) (i) the mistake was caused by information given by the other party; or
    (ii) the other party knew or ought to have known of the mistake and it was contrary to good faith and fair dealing to leave the mistaken party in error; or
    (iii) the other party made the same mistake,
and
(b) the other party knew or should have known that the mistaken party, had he known the truth, would not have entered the contract or would have done

so only on fundamentally different terms.
(2) However a party may not avoid the contract if
(a) in the circumstances his mistake was inexcusable, or
(b) the risk of the mistake was assumed, or in the circumstances should be borne, by him.

There is a separate article on allowing avoidance for fraud,[114] and one on incorrect information:

Incorrect information[115]
A party who has entered a contract relying on incorrect information given him by the other party to the contract may recover damages ... [on the reliance basis]... even if the information does not give rise to a fundamental mistake, unless the party who gave the information had reasonable grounds for believing that the information was true.

It will be seen that, on the one hand, the primary ground for avoidance of the contract is mistake, in accordance with the civil law model, rather than misrepresentation. The practical difference to English law is slight: avoidance will be possible if the resulting misapprehension is fundamental, or if there has been fraud.[116] Even if the misapprehension which results is not fundamental, the party who has been misled can recover damages if the other cannot disprove fault.[117]

On the other hand, the requirements for avoidance for mistake as to the substance have been made stricter than under French or German law. First, the mistake must be fundamental.[118] Second, the article follows a number of more modern civil codes in limiting relief to cases in which the other party has either caused the mistake, knows or should know of it or shares it.[119] This is aimed at strengthening the security of transactions.

Greater security than under French or German law is also provided in relation to mistakes over the terms of the contract. If one party makes a mistake, and the other says nothing though she knows what is meant, a separate draft article on interpretation will hold the latter to what the first party meant. In other cases, the mistaken party can avoid the contract only under the same conditions as for other kinds of mistake: in other words, the mistake must be fundamental and the other party must have known or have reason to know of it, or have caused it. There will be no relief if the mistake was inexcusable.

Reconciliation of the irreconcilable?

In contrast to English law, one party's acquiescence in the other's self-deception may give rise to a remedy, either avoidance for mistake (because the mistake is known to the other party) or, if there is an intention to deceive, avoidance and damages for fraud, which may include "fraudulent non-

39

disclosure". But in neither case is the obligation to point out the misapprehension absolute.

Cases like the *Poussin* case are criticised even by French lawyers[120] for discouraging the acquisition of valuable information by requiring it to be disclosed. Yet there are cases in which one party has acquired the knowledge at little or no cost and there is no good reason for him not to have to disclose it. The case of the seller of a house who does not point out to the buyer that it is infested with termites is an example.[121] More importantly, there are frequently situations in which it makes very good sense to impose a duty of disclosure on a party in relation to what she is selling, as opposed to requiring her to reveal facts about what she is buying.[122]

Thus probably neither the English nor the French rule is correct in all cases. What is appropriate cannot, in the present state of legal science, be laid down with precision. The Principles take the approach of applying a broad standard of good faith. For example, the Article on fraud makes a party liable for deliberate non-disclosure

> ...of any circumstance which according to reasonable standards of good faith and fair dealing he should have disclosed.

The German law which relies on the same principle has been justly criticised as vague.[123] The Principles therefore give further guidance as to the factors which seem relevant to what is required by good faith and fair dealing. The Comment states:

> In determining whether reasonable standards require disclosure of a particular fact, regard should be had to all the circumstances, including
> (a) whether the party alleged to be under a duty to disclose had special expertise;
> (b) the cost to him of acquiring the relevant information;
> (c) whether the other party could reasonably acquire the information for himself;
> (d) the apparent importance of the fact to the other party; and
> (e) the nature and circumstances of the contract.

If the apparent conflict in values is really a reflection of the different types of cases being dealt with by the various national systems, it should be possible for arbitrators and courts using guide-lines such as these to reach solutions which will receive support from both sides of the Channel. Perhaps the greatest strength of the newly emerging European contract law in its various forms is that it has the experience of more than a dozen legal systems to draw on in trying to fashion appropriate solutions to the many different cases which are likely to present themselves. And even if there are differing cultural attitudes, the law can play some role in developing a new, "European", culture.

Notes

1. See Beale (1993), 177-9.
2. Resolution of 26 May 1989, OJEC No. C 158/401 of 26 June 1989.
3. See Collins (1994), 232-4.
4. Collins (1994).
5. See further below.
6. I leave the question of competition law on one side.
7. The United Nations Convention on Contracts for the International Sale of Goods (Vienna, 1980) is also of great importance, but it is limited to sales and it does not deal with the full range of questions: e.g. validity (mistake, duress, etc.) is not covered.
8. Even this does not cover every topic a domestic contract book would deal with: e.g. lack of capacity, lack of authority and immorality or illegality are not covered: Art. 3.1.
9. The Commission and its working method are described in Beale (1993); Lando, O., "Principles of European Contract Law" (1992) 56 RabelsZ 261; Tallon, D., "Vers un Droit Européen du Contrat?" in *Mélanges offerts à André Colomer* (Litec, Paris, 1991).
10. Page xviii.
11. Art.1.101(3)(a).
12. In English law such an agreement will be upheld provided the resulting agreement is sufficiently certain, the choice is bona fide and not intended to evade the mandatory rules of the system, there is no illegality present and enforcement would not clearly be injurious to the public good: *Deutsche Schachtbau - und Tiefbohrgesellschaft mbH v Ras Al Khaimah National Oil Co* [1987] 3 W.L.R. 1023, CA.
13. Art. 1.101(3)(b).
14. For an example of the need for this see below, text before n. 67.
15. PECL, p.xviii.
16. It is always difficult to know where to draw this line. I have arbitrarily excluded Directives on company law, employment law and the protection of intellectual property; also those aimed at particular sectors such as banking, investment and insurance. A useful (though no longer up to date) list of Directives and published proposals will be found in P.-C. Müller-Graff,"Private Law Unification by Means other than of Codification", in Hartkamp, 19, pp.30-5.
17. Council Directive 86/653/EEC of 18 December 1986, OJ L 382 of 31.12.86, p.17, implemented by Commercial Agents (Council Directive) Regulations 1993 (SI 3053 1993). See Davis (1994) 144 New L.J. 388.
18. E.g. EC Directive 71/305 of 26 July 1971, OJ L 185 of 16.8.71, p.5 as amended by EC Directive 89/440 of 18 July 1989, OJ L 210 of 21.7.89, p.1 and implemented by Public Works Contracts Regulations

(SI 1991 No. 2680). A concise summary of the various provisions will be found in Croner's *Buying and Selling Law*, Part 6.

19. Council Directive 85/374/EEC of 25 July 1985, (OJ L 210 of 7.8.85, p.29); implemented by Consumer Protection Act 1987. Full discussions will be found in A. Clark, *Product Liability* (1989) and Stapleton.

20. Preamble, second paragraph.

21. Fifth paragraph.

22. Sixth and seventh paragraphs.

23. Treaty of European Union of December 1991, art.129a.

24. The changing bases of EC Consumer Policy are explored in S.Weatherill, "Aspects of the implementation of EC Consumer Law in the UK", paper delivered at the Conference on Approximation and Harmonisation of Law, Budapest, September 1995.

25. Council Directive on Contracts negotiated away from Business Premises, 85/577/EEC of 20 December 1985, OJ L372 of 31.12.85, p.31.

26. 87/102/EEC of 26 December 1986, OJ L42 of 12.2.87, p.48, am. by 90/88/EEC OJ L61 of 10.3.90, p.14.

27. See Stapleton, Chapter 3.

28. See particularly, Collins (1994); Macdonald, "Mapping UCTA and the UTCC Regulations" [1994] J. Business Law 441; Beale (1995).

29. I have suggested elsewhere that the provision for "public action" (under the Unfair Terms in Consumer Contracts Regulations 1994, to be taken by the Director-General of Fair Trading) may be of greater practical significance: Beale, "Unfair Contracts in Britain and Europe" [1989] Current Legal Problems 197, 210-2; Beale (1995), pp. 252-9.

30. Article 3.1. The term is to be judged by the circumstances at the time the contract was concluded, Article 4.1.

31. Department of Trade and Industry, *Implementation of the EC Directive on Unfair Terms in Consumer Contracts (93/13/EEC): A Further Consultation Document* (1994), Comment on Art. 3.1.

32. AGB-Gesetz, §9.1.

33. See G. Dannemann, *An Introduction to German Civil and Commercial Law* (1993), p.19; Beale (1995) at pp.242-5 and refs. cited therein. The fairness test is discussed in detail by R.Brownsword, G.Howells and T.Wilhelmsson, "Between Market and Welfare: Some Reflections on Article 3 of the EC Directive on Unfair Terms in Consumer Contracts", forthcoming in Willett.

34. Art.3.1.

35. See Collins (1994), p.238.

36. OJ C 73 of 23 March 1992, draft art.4; compare the exclusion of review of the price or terms defining the main subject matter of the contract by the final Directive, Art.4.2

37. COM(93)509 final, Brussels, 15 November 1993.

38.	Page 5.
39.	Page 9. Distortion of competition among vendors and manufacturers in different Member States is also referred to, e.g. at p.82.
40.	COM(92) 66 final - SYN 285, OJ C No. 73 of 24 March 1992, p.5.
41.	The draft Directive on Services has been withdrawn for further consideration.
42.	Green Paper, p.7.
43.	Green Paper, p.100.
44.	Pages 93-100.
45.	Compare DTI (1993) proposal 1, p.6; and see Beale (1996).
46.	Green Paper, p.87.
47.	This is explored in greater detail in Beale (1996).
48.	DTI (1993) proposal 3, p.9.
49.	First European Consumer Forum, Brussels, October 1994.
50.	17 May 1994.
51.	Mrs. Bonino made this announcement in May 1995. The draft may appear in the autumn of 1995.
52.	Article 2(b).
53.	Collins (1994), p. 240, points out that an individual trader making what is for her an unusual contract might be covered.
54.	I ignore the even more important question of what the rights may be worth in practice. The Commission is also conducting a project on access to justice. See Commission of the European Communities, Green Paper: Access of Consumers to Justice and the Settlement of Consumer Disputes in the Single Market, COM(93) 576 final, Brussels 16 November 1993.
55.	Collins (1994) pp. 235-6 and 240.
56.	This is nowhere more obvious than in the discussion of the "commercial guarantee" noted earlier: should these merely have to make it clear what is being offered or should there be a minimum content?
57.	Section 3 (England and Wales); section 17 (Scotland).
58.	Sections 6(3) and 7(3) (England and Wales); ss.20(2)(b)(ii) and 20(1)(a)(ii) (Scotland).
59.	See Beale (1995), p.246.
60.	Subject to the rules of mitigation and remoteness of damage.
61.	The manufacturer is already responsible for personal injury to the consumer and damage to her property over 500 ECU under the Directive on Liability for Defective Products of 25 July 1985.
62.	See further Beale (1996).
63.	Code Civil, art.1645; Nicholas, p.82.
64.	See above, text at n. 40.
65.	Pages 89-90.
66.	In Arts. 4.501-4.509. Almost all the rules will be readily recognised by Common Lawyers.

67. Some of the difficulties mentioned have arisen in drafting Part I of the
     Principles. These are explored in Beale (1993), pp.184-94. However
     they seem much less serious than those relating to misapprehensions.

68. This must be the starting point for a comparative and synthetic exercise
     of this kind: see Zweigert & Kötz pp.31 ff.

69. As in e.g, *Dick Bentley Productions Ltd v Harold Smith Motors Ltd*
     [1965] 1 W.L.R. 623.

70. The misrepresentation must be material, but this appears to exclude
     only something which would not have influenced the reasonable person,
     cf. Marine Insurance Act 1906, s.18(2).

71. Misrepresentation Act 1967, s.2(2).

72. Misrepresentation Act 1967, s.2(1). Damages may also be recovered at
     common law under the doctrine of negligent misstatement, see *Esso
     Petroleum Co Ltd v Mardon* [1976] Q.B. 801, but this requires the
     plaintiff to show that there was a "special relationship" between the
     parties and to prove negligence, so the remedy under the Act is more
     useful.

73. E.g. *Hartog v Colin & Shields* [1939] 3 All E.R. 566.

74. For this purpose we can ignore any differences beytween the doctrines
     of common mistake at common law, see *Bell v Lever Bros Ltd* [1932]
     A.C. 161, and in equity, see *Solle v Butcher* [1950] 1 K.B. 671.

75. Section 14(2).

76. Section 14(3). There is no implied term if the buyer did not rely, or it
     was unreasonable for him to rely, on the seller's skill and judgment.

77. There are special provisions for the sale of buildings in the course of
     construction: Civil Code arts. 1601-1 ff.

78. See Treitel, *Law of Contract* (9th ed, 1995), pp.318-9.

79. *Bannerman v White* (1861) 10 C.B.N.S. 844.

80. *Dick Bentley Productions Ltd v Harold Smith Motors Ltd* [1965] 1
     W.L.R. 623, cf *Oscar Chess Ltd v Williams* [1957] 1 W.L.R. 370
     (maker of statement less expert than other party).

81. Nicholas, p.113. The section which follows is heavily indebted to this
     book. Professor Denis Tallon has also provided me with information.

82. CC Art. 1110.

83. See Malaurie & Aynès, §410; Nicholas, p.91.

84. Civ. 17.11.1930, S.1932.1.17, DP 1932.1.161, Gaz.Pal 1930.2.1031.

85. *The Villa Jacqueline* case, Civ. 23.11.1931, DP 1932.1.129, n.
     Josserand.

86. See Nicholas, pp.92-4. It has been argued that, when a matter is not
     obviously determining, the debate is really one about the burden of
     proof of its importance: Malaurie & Aynès, §406.

87. *Bell v Lever Bros Ltd* [1932] A.C. 161; *Solle v Butcher* [1950] 1 K.B.
     671. The new Civil Code of the Netherlands seems even closer to the
     English test for misrepresentation. An error imputable to information

given by the other party is a ground for relief "unless the other party could assume that the contract would have been entered into even without this information": (BW 6:228(1)(a)).

88. BGB §119(2).
89. Witz §336. I have drawn heavily on this work. I am also very grateful to Professor Ulrich Drobnig for furnishing information.
90. BGH 26.10.1978, NJW 1979, 160, 161.
91. Witz, §343
92. But not exceeding the expectation interest.
93. See Witz, §§354-7.
94. Malaurie & Aynès, §875; Nicholas, pp. 110-1, citing eg Civ. 29.11.1968, Gaz.Pal. 1969.1.63.
95. See Witz, §373.
96. RG 22.12.1905, RGZ 62, 205; RG 28.9.1916, RGZ 88,411.
97. In French law claims of mistake are often made even when the buyer would have a remedy for non-performance or on the *garantie*: see Nicholas, p.113. In German law, a buyer may not seek relief for mistake if she has remedies for latent defect under BGB §§459 ff. See Witz, §346 ff.
98. *The Nai Genova* [1984] 1 Lloyd's Rep. 353, 365; *Commission for New Towns v Cooper (GB) Ltd, The Times*, 3 March 1995.
99. See Nicholas, pp.98-100.
100. See Witz, §§323-4.
101. BGB §120.
102. For reasons of space I ignore the possibility that situations involving misapprehensions may in these systems sometimes be dealt with under other doctrines; e.g. in French law *cause* or *objet*, in German law initial impossibility and *clausula rebus sic stantibus*.
103. See Nicholas, pp 102-6; J.Ghestin, "The Pre-Contractual Obligation to Disclose Information: French Report" in Harris and Tallon, p.151; P. LeGrand, "Pre-contractual Disclosure and Information: English and French Law Compared", (1986) 6 Oxford J. Legal Studies 322; M.Fabre-Magnan (1995).
104. RG 7.7.1925, RGZ 111, 233, 234.
105. BGH 8.1.1959, BGHZ 29, 148, 150.
106. OLG Celle, 6.11.1970, MDR 1971, 392.
107. Many writers have made this or similar points: eg Nicholas, p.100; van Rossum, "Defects of Consent and Capacity in Contract Law" in Hartkamp, 135, p.136.
108. See Nicholas, p.114; Harris and Tallon, p.385.
109. "European Private Law and the Cultural Identity of States", forthcoming, European Review of Private Law. I am very grateful to Professor Collins for sending me an advance copy of this piece.
110. See also ibid., p.386.

111. Civ. 13.2.1983, D. 1984.340, JCP 1984.II.20186; Versailles 7.1.1987, D. 1987.485, Gaz.Pal. 1987.34. A fuller account will be found in Nicholas, p.87.
112. See Nicholas, p.105; Rudden, *"Le juste et l'inefficace; pour un devoir de non-renseignements"* Rev. Tr. Dr. Civ. 1985, 91-103. On the general argument that a rule requiring disclosure of information which it was costly to acquire see A.Kronman, "Mistake, Disclosure, Information and the Law of Contracts" (1978) 7 J. Legal Studies 1.
113. Currently numbered 6.103. When the Principles are re-issued as a whole they will be re-numbered.
114. Currently 6.107.
115. Currently 6.106.
116. Cf. Misrepresentation Act 1967, s.2(2).
117. Cf. Misrepresentation Act 1967, s.2(1).
118. Here the equivalent UNIDROIT Article, 3.5, differs, referring to "material". This word was avoided by PECL as possibly ambiguous - does it mean serious or merely non-trivial? Otherwise the PECL and UNIDROIT articles are very similar, save that the UNIDROIT version also allows avoidance if "the other party had not at the time of avoidance acted in reliance on the contract." That was not adopted by PECL as it does not seem to be reflected in any of the laws of the Member States.
119. Cf. the new Netherlands BW 6:228 and Italian CC Art 1431. See also the suggestion in Zweigert & Kötz, p.452.
120. M.Fabre-Magnan, p.116.
121. *Obde v Schlemeyer* 56 Wash. 2d 449, 353 P. 2d 672 (1960).
122. M.Fabre-Magnan, pp.116-20, argues convincingly that a duty to disclose facts about the value of one's own *prestation* (i.e. the object of one's obligation) is not inefficient.
123. Witz, §359.

Bibliography

Beale, H. (1993): "Towards a Law of Contract for Europe: the Work of the Commission on European Contract Law" in G.Weick (ed.), *National and European Law on the Threshold to the Single Market*, p.177.

Beale, H. (1995): "Legislative Control of Fairness: The Directive on Unfair Terms in Consumer Contracts" in Beatson, below, p.231.

Beale, H. (1996): "Customers, Chains and Networks" in Willett, below.

Beatson, J. and Friedmann, D. (eds), *Good faith and fault in Contract Law* (Clarendon Press, Oxford, 1995).

Collins, H. (1994): "Good Faith in European Contract Law" 14 Oxford J Legal Studies 229.

DTI (1993): Department of Trade and Industry, *Consumer Guarantees: A Consultation Document*.

Fabre-Magnan, M.: "Duties of Disclosure and French Contract Law" in Beatson (above), p.99.

Green Paper: Commission of the European Communities, *Green Paper on Guarantees for Consumer Goods and After-sales Services*, COM(93)509 final, Brussels, 15 November 1993.

Harris, D. and Tallon, D. (ed.s) *Contract Law Today* (Oxford University Press, 1989).

Hartkamp, A. and others (eds) *Towards a European Civil Code* (Ars Aequi Libri, Nijmegen, 1994).

Malaurie, P. & Aynès, L: *Droit Civil, Les Obligations* (5th ed., Éditions Cujas, Paris, 1994).

Nicholas, B.: *French Law of Contract* (2nd ed., Clarendon Press, Oxford, 1992).

PECL: Commission on European Contract Law, *Principles of European Contract Law, Part I: Performance, Non-performance and Remedies* (eds Lando and Beale) (Martinus Nijhoff, Dordrecht, 1995).

Stapleton, J.: *Product Liability* (Butterworths, London, 1994).

UNIDROIT: *Principles of International Commercial Contracts* (International Institute for the Unification of Private Law, Rome, 1994).

Willett, C. (ed.), *Fairness in Contract* (forthcoming 1996, E.Elgar).

Witz, C. *Droit Privé Allemand: 1. Actes juridiques, droits subjectifs* (Litec, Paris, 1992).

Zweigert, K. & Kötz, H.: *Introduction to Comparative Law* (Clarendon Press, Oxford, 1992).

3   Static and Dynamic Market Individualism

ROGER BROWNSWORD

Introduction

Legislation might be said to be "ideological" in more than one sense. In a pejorative sense, legislation might be described (and, by implication, criticised) as "ideological" where it is perceived to serve a particular political dogma without giving due weight to the requirements of the public interest, or where it is accompanied by rhetoric that masks or misrepresents the nature of the regulation, or the like. In another (non-pejorative) sense, however, all legislation is ideological, meaning simply that it is guided by a set of ideas about how social, legal, and economic life should be organised. To this extent, recent legislative reforms of, say, the criminal justice system—from the Police and Criminal Evidence Act 1984 through to the Criminal Justice and Public Order Act 1994—are as much ideological as the Conservative government's regulation of the trade unions (see e.g. Fredman, 1992) or its programmes of privatisation, marketisation, and contractualisation (see e.g. Graham and Prosser, 1987; Harden, 1992).

In principle, where legislation concerns matters of contract law, it might be said to be ideological in either the pejorative or the non-pejorative sense—indeed, it *must be* ideological in the latter sense. For example, the recent Unfair Terms in Consumer Contracts Regulations 1994 (implementing the EC Directive on Unfair Terms in Consumer Contracts), although not politically contentious nor backed by any conspicuous political dogma, fairly clearly enacts a scheme of values relating to the protection of consumer contractors. Similarly, the Sale and Supply of Goods Act 1994 strikes a fresh balance between the interests of sellers and buyers, involving judgments *inter alia* about how far purchasers should be protected against minor defects in goods and how far sellers should be protected

48

against opportunistic rejections by commercial buyers. Such legislation, in other words, like all legislation, is ideological in the non-pejorative sense.

Much of contract law, however, is based in case-law rather than legislation and, to this extent, it enjoys some immunity against political influence. Does it follow, therefore, that the case-law of contract is not ideological in the non-pejorative sense? The short answer is that it does not so follow. For, the ideological underpinning of the law of contract derives not from its increasingly legislative source but from the simple fact that law (whether originating in political or judicial institutions) is purposive in its nature. Where there are purposes there necessarily are valued end states—there necessarily are ideologies in the non-pejorative sense.

The leading doctrines of the case-law of contract in England reflect two principal ideologies, "market-individualism" and "consumer-welfarism" (see Adams and Brownsword, 1987, 1994). Putting the contrast very generally, whereas the former ideology insists upon contractors being held to their freely agreed exchanges, the latter seeks to ensure a fair deal for consumer contractors and, more generally, to relieve against harsh or unconscionable bargains. Because the case-law of contract is determined in an adjudicative context, however, we must reckon with a second layer of ideological complexity. All adjudication, in all branches of law, is caught up in a tension between an ideology of "formalism" (which dictates that the settled law should be applied, the precedents followed, and so on) and an ideology of "realism" (which, at its most robust, demands that cases should be determined according to their merits, settled law notwithstanding) (see Adams and Brownsword, 1992). In practice, this double layering of ideological tensions generates three strands in judicial reasoning—first, a formalist regard for applying the law, secondly a market-individualist brand of realism with an emphasis on calculability and holding contractors to their bargains, and thirdly a consumer-welfarist brand of realism concerned with protecting consumers against sharp practice and generally relieving against unconscionable deals.

The purpose of this chapter is to draw a distinction between two versions of market-individualism, which we can term "static" and "dynamic" market-individualism. Although both versions of market-individualism take the process of contracting to be an essentially self-interested activity, with a freely agreed exchange as the paradigm, they rest on rather different bases. Static market-individualism is a fully detached or independent ideology: it has a particular vision of the purpose of contract and how transactions should be regulated; it imposes this view on the contracting community; and, in this sense, it "constitutes" the market. By contrast, the ideology of dynamic market-individualism is to a considerable extent dependent, reflecting the practice and expectations of the contracting community (particularly the business community). It follows that, as the practice and the views of the contracting community change, the ideology of dynamic market-individualism moves to track these changes. To this extent, therefore, dynamic market-individualism is less than fully constitutive of the market.

The principal analysis in this chapter is presented in three sections: first, the contrast between static and dynamic market-individualism is elaborated; secondly, in the light of this contrast, a number of recent decisions are reviewed; and, thirdly, the implications of the distinction between these two versions of market-individualist ideology are considered. Essentially, the distinction is significant in three connected respects: first, because it facilitates a clearer mapping of doctrinal developments in contract law; secondly, because it points to a critical question for any theory of contract law that takes the concept of legitimate or reasonable expectation as one of its cornerstones—namely, whether the reference point (or criterion) for such expectations is the custom, practice, and opinion of the contracting community or some independent theory of legitimate interests; and, thirdly, because it captures the nature of the transformation of the classical law into a modern commercial law of contract.

Static and dynamic market-individualism contrasted

Market-individualism, whether static or dynamic, is an ideology with two aspects, a market and an individualistic aspect. To draw the contrast between static and dynamic market-individualism, we can work first through the market dimension of each version of the ideology and then through their individualistic aspects.

(1) The market dimension

Static market-individualism sees the principal function of contract law as being to establish a clear set of ground rules within which a market can operate. To this extent, contract law is constitutive of the market. Markets, of course, may operate with all sorts of ground rules, customs and practices (cf. Daintith, 1993). In some markets, a nod and a wink may be sufficient to close a deal; in others, the deal is not closed until the sealing wax has dried on the contractual documents. For the static market-individualist, the distinctive contribution of the English law of contract is to declare the conventions in such a way that all those who deal in the contract-constituted market place know exactly where they stand.

Three of the most important ground rules concern formation (i.e. at what moment the parties are bound), third-party effects, and remedies for breach. Here, static market-individualism develops its rules around two key concepts, exchange and expectation (cf. Eisenberg, 1981-82). First, the (formation) rule is that a contract comes into existence when, and only when, the terms of an exchange have been fully specified and freely agreed upon. Secondly, only those who deal as parties to the exchange can take the benefit of the contract (or be burdened by its terms). And, thirdly, the basic remedial rule is that, where there is a breach, the innocent party's expectation of performance (by the contract-breaker) is to be protected—generally speaking, by damages or an action for the agreed price rather than by a decree of specific performance as such.

These ground rules have the virtue of drawing bright lines (between situations where a binding contract is in place and where it is not, between those who can sue on a particular contract and those who cannot, and so on). However, the rules do not always generate results that seem entirely reasonable. Examples of such hard cases are legion: for instance, cases where an expected contract does not eventuate and one side incurs significant (anticipatory) reliance costs, cases where an agreed variation of a contract does not qualify as an exchange, cases where an intended third-party beneficiary is unable to enforce a contract, cases where the expectation measure of compensation seems over-generous, and so on. Now, although it can be argued in response to such hard cases that the results are simply in line with the constitutive rules, and that these rules are well-known, this does not assist where significant numbers in both the commercial and the legal communities feel uneasy with these outcomes.

Dynamic market-individualism responds to these difficulties by favouring a more flexible approach, guided by the practices and expectations of the contracting community (particularly the commercial community). Accordingly, the paradigms of static market-individualism remain central but they are qualified in significant ways. For example, if the commercial community favours protection in certain situations for pre-contractual reliance, enforcement of agreed variations (even though they might be one-sided), recognition of third-party interests, and the like, then dynamic market-individualism argues that the law should run with the grain of opinion. A textbook statement of such sentiments can be found in Lord Wilberforce's well-known remarks in *The Eurymedon*[1] (where, it will be recalled, the point at issue was whether the stevedore third-parties were entitled to rely on protective provisions in the main carriage contract):

> The whole contract is of a commercial character, involving service on one side, rates of payment on the other, and qualifying stipulations as to both. The relations of all parties to each other are commercial relations entered into for business reasons of ultimate profit. To describe one set of promises in this context as gratuitous, or *nudum pactum*, seems paradoxical and is *prima facie* implausible. It is only the precise analysis of this complex of relations into the classical offer and acceptance, with identifiable consideration, that seems to present difficulty, but this same difficulty exists in many situations of daily life, e.g. sales at auction; supermarket purchases; boarding an omnibus; purchasing a train ticket; tenders for the supply of goods; offers of rewards; acceptance by post; warranties of authority by agents; manufacturers' guarantees; gratuitous bailments; bankers' commercial credits. These are all examples which show that English law, having committed itself to a rather technical and schematic doctrine of contract, in application takes a practical approach, often at the cost of

51

forcing the facts to fit uneasily into the marked slots of offer, acceptance and consideration.[2]

Similarly, in the more recent case of *G. Percy Trentham Ltd. v. Archital Luxfer Ltd.*,[3] which concerned a battle of the forms problem, the Court of Appeal recognised that a contract could come into existence in stages, without there being a particular moment at which a comprehensive offer was definitively accepted and a contract (as classically conceived) materialised. As Steyn LJ put it, the courts "ought not to yield to Victorian times in realism about the practical application of rules of contract formation."[4] In other words, if (in *The Eurymedon*) the understanding of contractors involved in the carriage of goods by sea is that the protection of carriage contracts normally extends to the stevedores who unload the goods, and if (in the *Trentham* case) the understanding of contractors involved in the construction industry is that they have a contractual relationship under which work has actually been carried out (and, in fact, in *Trentham* itself, completed), then classical contract doctrine must be repositioned to accommodate such commercial expectations (cf. Buckley, 1993; Eisenberg, 1995).

(2) The individualist dimension

For the static market-individualist, the law of contract should set up a stable framework within which contractors can agree to exchanges that promise to maximise their individual utility. Contractors, on this view, are licensed to act as self-interested utility maximisers and, having so acted, they are required by the principle of sanctity of contract to respect the bargains that they have struck. However, the market-individualist view of contract as a freely agreed exchange imposes some constraints on the unbridled pursuit of self-interest. In particular, the law of contract must regulate against fraud and coercion, the former because it undermines the reality of agreement, the latter because it is inconsistent with the notion of a *free* transaction. For present purposes, the question of whether or not there is ultimately any coherent deep justification for these minimal restrictions on the advancement of self-interest need not trouble us (cf. Kronman, 1980). Rather, what we should note is the importance to static market-individualism that the regulation of fraud and coercion should respect two principles: first, that the lines between fraud and non-fraud, and between coercion and non-coercion, should be drawn clearly so that the ground rules for contracting remain bright and sharp; and, secondly, that the lines should be drawn in such a position that they offer no encouragement to contractors who, having made bad bargains, are looking for excuses for non-performance.

When we turn to dynamic market-individualism, we find the paradigms of market-individualism—contracting as self-interested dealing; contract as exchange; contract as free agreement—qualified by commercial practice and opinion. One conspicuous example of such qualification can be seen in the adoption of an overriding requirement of good faith in the performance and enforcement of contracts. Thus, in his seminal paper on the good faith provisions of the Uniform Commercial Code, E. Allan Farnsworth (1962-63) argued that the criterion of good faith should be constituted by reasonable commercial standards of fair dealing in the trade. Similarly, in the Australian case of *Renard Constructions (ME) Property Ltd. v. Minister for Public Works*,[5] Priestley JA said:

> [P]eople generally, including judges and other lawyers, from all strands of the community, have grown used to the courts applying standards of fairness to contract which are wholly consistent with the existence in all contracts of a duty upon the parties of good faith and fair dealing in its performance. In my view this is in these days the expected standard, and *anything less is contrary to prevailing community expectations.*[6]

In other words, there is a general expectation that contractors should deal fairly and act in good faith which crystallises into more specific views about how far self-interested opportunism, shirking, manipulation and the like, should be restricted. Of course, the expectations of commercial contractors might fluctuate and, indeed, might reflect underlying economic pressures. For example, we might find that commercial opinion expects quite high levels of co-operation where trading conditions are stable but that its expectation of co-operation is significantly lower where the economy is in recession (cf. Galanter and Rogers, 1988; Vincent-Jones, 1993). At all events, the dynamic market-individualist will judge it appropriate that the law should follow the general drift of commercial expectation whether it be relatively restrictive or relatively permissive in relation to contractors prioritising their self-interest.

The concept of free agreement, too, may be qualified in a dynamic market-individualist regime. For example, whereas static market-individualism takes a transaction as being freely made in the absence of very obvious forms of coercion, dynamic market-individualism must make provision for those more subtle forms of pressure that commercial opinion regards as improper. Such provision could be made within the terms of a broad-ranging good faith requirement. In the modern English law of contract, however, provision has been made in the form of a doctrine of economic duress. Ever since the landmark decision in *The Atlantic Baron*,[7] when the doctrine was first accepted, there has been a difficult question about how the line is to be drawn between economic duress and legitimate commercial pressure. Naturally, for the static market-individualist, such doctrinal indeterminacy is a cause for concern. However, for the dynamic market-individualist, such indeterminacy is a mark of doctrinal sophistication as the law attempts to be more sensitive to commercial opinion.

Another example of the law taking a harder look at whether agreement is free can be found in the modern regulation of unfair terms. For static market-individualists, there are obvious dangers in conferring a judicial discretion to strike out unreasonable terms. However, for dynamic market-individualists such a discretion (as ever guided by commercial opinion) may be justifiable where the terms have not been freely agreed. Now, the modern market place involves a vast amount of routine standardised transacting, in relation to which it is hardly sensible to talk about free agreement in the sense of freely negotiated agreement. However, where commercial opinion accepts that not every deal can be individually negotiated, the harder look at unfair terms is focused somewhere above this threshold of acceptable standard dealing. In other words, the commercial community accepts that standardised dealing makes for efficiency and that, within the bounds of such dealing, there are various kinds of terms (or arrangements of terms) that would pass as normal. However, where particular terms stand out as abnormal, a question is raised about whether such terms have been freely agreed and the onus passes to the party seeking to rely on such terms to demonstrate that they were freely agreed upon. There are a number of doctrinal expressions of this idea but, in England, the "reasonableness requirement" of the Unfair Contract Terms Act 1977 is the most significant double-check on whether agreement has been genuinely free.

In the light of this sketch of the contrast between static and dynamic market-individualism, we can look for some of these ideological imprints in a selection of decisions drawn from the recent case-law.

Recent case-law

One of the pillars of static market-individualism is the idea that contract is constituted by exchange. Where there is no exchange, there is no contract. From this simple idea, two doctrinal consequences of enormous importance follow. First, it follows that there is no contract where the parties have not yet reached the moment of exchange (even though they are working towards it). And, secondly, it follows that, even though the parties are already joined by an exchange, there is no fresh contract where the terms are modified without there being a fresh exchange. In the recent case-law, these consequences (and the central idea itself) have been significantly qualified by two major decisions of the Court of Appeal, the *Blackpool and Fylde Aero Club*[8] case and *Williams v. Roffey Bros. and Nicholls (Contractors) Ltd.*[9]

The specific question raised by the *Blackpool and Fylde Aero Club* case was whether the club could hold the defendant council to its advertised procedures for the consideration of tenders submitted in relation to a local airport concession. Given that the club, in submitting its tender, was merely making an offer which the council was free to reject, did the law of contract give the tendering contractors any protection? In an interesting ruling, the Court of Appeal held that there was a degree of protection. According to Sir Thomas Bingham, the council was not free to ignore its own published tendering guidelines (e.g. by accepting a tender well before the deadline for tenders to be submitted had been reached, or by accepting a tender received well after the deadline) otherwise "there would in my view be an unacceptable discrepancy between the law of contract and the confident assumptions of commercial parties."[10] Moreover, in holding that the club's understanding of the tendering process raised an entitlement, "not as a matter of mere expectation but of contractual right",[11] that the council should abide by its own rules, the court followed the line taken in a number of other jurisdictions that the law of contract is capable of giving at least some protection to the interests of commercial parties who are working their way towards an exchange.[12]

If the *Blackpool and Fylde Aero Club* case breaks new ground in relation to pre-contractual reliance and expectation, *Williams v. Roffey Bros. and Nicholls (Contractors) Ltd.* follows suit in relation to reliance and expectation encouraged during the performance of a contract. As is well known, the question in *Williams v. Roffey* was whether the main contractors were contractually bound by their promise to pay the carpenter sub-contractors *additional* sums (over and above the agreed contractual price) for the contract work. In holding that the main contractors were so bound, provided that their promise was freely given and procured some practical advantage to the promisors, the Court of Appeal departed from the settled principle that A's promise to perform (or the actual performance of) his existing contractual duty to B is no consideration for a promise by B to pay additional sums to A (see Adams and Brownsword, 1990a; Halson, 1990). Although the decision gives rise to a host of doctrinal concerns (see Chen-Wishart, 1995), for present purposes, we need not agonise about whether it is better to say that the Court of Appeal revised the traditional concept of an "exchange" (as embedded in the English doctrine of consideration) or simply that it effectively dispensed with the requirement of an exchange for a binding variation within an existing contractual relationship—for, either way, the Court must be seen as taking its lead from the expectations of commercial contractors rather than from the classical rule-book associated with the static form of market-individualism.[13]

With the weakening of the consideration requirement, we might also expect some qualification of the privity doctrine. In both Canada and Australia, there have been some important head-on confrontations with the privity principle (particularly invited by the involvement of many contracting parties in commercial projects such as construction and carriage: see Adams and Brownsword, 1990b, and 1993); and, in England, the most recent case-law takes place in the knowledge that the Law Commission (1991) has provisionally recommended legislative reform of the doctrine. So, for example, in both *The Pioneer Container*[14] and *White v. Jones*,[15] we find Lord Goff remarking that it is now open to question how long the basic privity principles will be maintained in all their strictness. Perhaps the most interesting recent case in this area, however, is that of the Court of Appeal in *Darlington Borough Council v. Wiltshier Northern Limited*.[16] The essential dispute in this case concerned alleged defects in a building, the Dolphin Centre, built for Darlington by Wiltshier. However, before this dispute could be settled, a preliminary issue arose: namely, even if Wiltshier were in breach of the building contract, would Darlington be entitled to recover substantial damages? This preliminary question arose because Darlington were not actually a party to the building contract—to avoid (quite lawfully) the borrowing constraints of the Local Government Act 1972, Darlington financed the deal via Morgan Grenfell who thus became parties to the building contract with Wiltshier. However, as Steyn L.J. emphasised, the building contract was for the benefit of Darlington and there was no doubt that "that is how all three parties saw it".[17] Accordingly, but for the doctrine of privity of contract, Darlington could simply have sued on the contract made for its benefit.

Given that there was *de facto* a tripartite arrangement here—which, to repeat Steyn L.J.'s emphasis, was how the parties themselves saw it—the privity doctrine involved breaking up the contracts in a somewhat artificial way (particularly bearing in mind that the benefit of the building contract had been duly assigned to Darlington by Morgan Grenfell). Ignoring privity, one might simply have argued that Darlington had a free-standing direct claim on the building contract. However, the court took a less radical step, holding that, in principle, Morgan Grenfell could have claimed substantial damages (even though they suffered no loss) and so Darlington, as assignees, had a similar claim. In so holding, the court adopted the approach ventured by the House of Lords in *Linden Gardens Trust Ltd. v. Lenesta Sludge Disposals Ltd.*[18] according to which there are, exceptionally, some circumstances in which a plaintiff may recover damages for the benefit of a third party—quite what those circumstances are remains to be fully determined, but the underlying idea is that the exception will apply to provide "a remedy where no other would be available to a person sustaining loss which under a rational legal system ought to be compensated by the person who has caused it."[19]

The question of what a rational legal system might require is, of course, a large and controversial matter (see Brownsword, 1993; Adams and Brownsword, 1995). In the context of the *Darlington* case, however, it is pretty clear that a rational system will not tolerate a meritorious claim falling down some doctrinal black-hole, as counsel put it,[20] not least where such an outcome flaws reasonable commercial expectations.

Before we turn from the traces of dynamic market-individualism evident in the recent case-law, one more recent decision merits a mention. This is the decision of the Court of Appeal in the *BSkyB* case.[21] The dispute in this case arose out of a number of agreements made in 1989 and 1990 between British Satellite Broadcasting (BSB) and Philips at the time that BSB and Sky were locked in competition to control the satellite television market in the UK. By late 1990, BSB had lost the battle and had merged with Sky. One of the results of this merger was that Philips, who had contracted with BSB to develop and manufacture receivers for the BSB system, were left with unsold stock, surplus manufacturing capacity, and no continuing opportunity to sell the receivers. Philips tried to recoup their losses by arguing that BSB were in breach of various implied terms of their agreements, but particularly an implied term to the effect that BSB "would not commit any act which would tend to impede or render impossible the marketing of the Receivers and/or to render the Receivers useless or unmarketable". Although Philips persuaded the trial judge that such an implied term was part of the agreement, they failed before the Court of Appeal. According to Sir Thomas Bingham MR:[22]

> Had the parties addressed their minds at the outset to the eventuality that the operation turned out to be a major commercial flop, it is by no means clear how they would have agreed that the risk should be allocated or, if they had agreed that Philips should be protected, what form they would have agreed that that protection should take. It seems likely that there would have been tough negotiation, with Philips seeking maximum protection and BSB conceding the minimum.

Now, whilst Sir Thomas's remarks presuppose that the parties would have been eager to have protected their own commercial interests, he went on to say:[23]

> For the avoidance of doubt we should add that we would, were it material, imply a term that BSB should act with good faith in the performance of this contract.

However, as the Court ruled, it was not in fact material for there was no suggestion that BSB acted in bad faith in entering into the merger with Sky and no more extended concept of good faith was relied upon. Nevertheless, the explicit recognition by the Court of Appeal of a duty to act in good faith in the performance of a commercial contract is the sign of a court ready to move from the static to the dynamic market-individualist approach.

If the recent case-law bears some imprints of dynamic market-individualist thinking, it equally bears the continuing imprint of static market-individualism. Three illustrations will suffice: *Walford v. Miles*,[24] *Regalian Properties plc v. London Dockland Development Corp.*,[25] and *Re Selectmove Ltd.*[26]

In *Walford v. Miles*, as is well known, the House of Lords emphatically rejected the suggestion from the Court of Appeal that English law might recognise the validity of an agreement to negotiate in good faith. In a particularly striking speech, Lord Ackner proclaimed:[27]

> [T]he concept of a duty to carry on negotiations in good faith is inherently repugnant to the adversarial position of the parties when involved in negotiations. Each party to the negotiations is entitled to pursue his (or her) own interest, so long as he avoids making misrepresentations...A duty to

negotiate in good faith is as unworkable in practice as it is inherently inconsistent with the position of a negotiating party.

Whilst, therefore, English law recognises the validity of clearly defined "lock-out" agreements, it does not recognise the validity of "lock-in" agreements even when backed by an understanding that negotiations are to be conducted in good faith, or that the parties should make best efforts to agree, or something of that kind. For orthodox contract lawyers, not only are such agreements too uncertain to enforce, they are at odds (as Lord Ackner reminds us) with the adversarial ethic that is the underpinning of static market-individualism.[28]

The thinking in *Walford v. Miles* indicates that contractors are largely expected to look after their own interests during the negotiation of a contract. At this stage, the risk is not simply that one's fellow negotiator might prefer to close the deal with a third-party (as in *Walford v. Miles* itself); for, even if no third-party is involved, an expected contract may fail to eventuate, leaving the negotiating party with considerable pre-contractual expenses. Such a situation arose in *Regalian Properties plc v. London Dockland Development Corp.* There, in Summer 1986, Regalian had entered into an agreement "subject to contract" with London Dockland Development Corporation for a proposed residential development of land in Wapping. Some two years later, for a variety of reasons, the contract had not been finalised—in part, this was because of difficulties in securing vacant possession of the whole of the site, in part, it was because the fluctuations in land values prompted a number of reviews of the price to be paid by Regalian. At all events, by late 1988, the slump in the residential property market was such that Regalian realised that it would be unwise to proceed with the project and negotiations between the parties duly lapsed. The question to which the failed negotiations gave rise was whether Regalian were entitled to be reimbursed by London Dockland Development Corporation for just under £2.9m spent on professional fees (particularly architects' fees in respect of preparing the designs) in pursuance of the agreement "subject to contract" and in anticipation of the contract itself.

Regalian pleaded their claim for reimbursement in restitution, conceding that there could be no straightforward contractual action on an agreement "subject to contract". The restitutionary claim, however, was no more straightforward, for Rattee J. declined to hold that Regalian's expenses were incurred for the benefit of London Dockland Development Corporation—rather, the expenses were incurred with a view to putting Regalian into a position to start work on the development if and when the contract was finalised. This left Regalian to clutch at the principle of good faith, particularly as applied in this context by Sheppard J. in *Sabemo Pty. Ltd. v. North Sydney Municipal Council*,[29] the gist of which is that negotiating parties are to be protected where one party "unilaterally decides to abandon the project, not for any reason associated with bona fide disagreement concerning the terms of the contract to be entered into, but for reasons which, however valid, pertain only to his own position and do not relate at all to that of the other party." Rattee J. ruled that this principle was not applicable on the facts, because the Corporation had not unilaterally abandoned the project. More significantly, however, he suggested that the *Sabemo* principle should not be extended to situations where the parties realised that they incurred negotiation costs at their own risk:

> I appreciate that the English law of restitution should be flexible and capable of continuous development. However, I see no good reason to extend it to apply some such principle as adopted by Sheppard J in the *Sabemo* case to facts such as those of the present case, where, however much the parties expect a contract between them to materialise, both enter negotiations expressly...on terms that each party is free to withdraw from the negotiations at any time. Each party to such negotiations must be taken to know...that pending the conclusion of a binding contract any cost incurred by him in preparation for the intended contract will be incurred at his own risk in the sense that he will have no recompense for those costs if no contract results.[30]

Although it was agreed in *Regalian* that negotiations covered by the rubric "subject to contract", entailed that either party "was free to walk away from [the] negotiations, however little [the other party] expected it to do so",[31] there is an important difference in principle between walking away for any reason whatsoever and walking away for a reason that keeps faith with the integrity of the negotiating situation. What Sheppard J sought to draw out in the *Sabemo* case was just this point, that a bad faith withdrawal from negotiations (just like a bad faith withdrawal from a concluded contract) is defined by the reasons motivating that withdrawal (cf. Brownsword, 1992 and 1994a; Burton, 1980-81)—which, of course, is not to say that an inquiry into a party's reasons for withdrawal will always prove to be straightforward in practice (see, e.g., Cohen, 1995). Whereas static market-individualist thinking prefers to cling to the certainties supposedly associated with key doctrinal signals—such as "subject to contract" or, in the context of withdrawal for breach, breach of "condition"—it is distinctive of dynamic market-individualist thinking that the law should attempt to track the way in which commercial people themselves discriminate between legitimate and illegitimate reasons for action.

The final case to be considered in this short review of some recent developments is *Re Selectmove*, where the principal question was whether the Inland Revenue was bound by a promise allegedly made that it would allow Selectmove Ltd. to pay off tax arrears at a rate of £1,000 a month. At first instance, it was held that, in the absence of any consideration moving from the company to the Revenue for this concession, the promise was not contractually binding—indeed, given the decision of the House of Lords in *Foakes v Beer*,[32] such was trite law. On appeal, counsel for the company argued that, in the light of the reasoning in *Williams v Roffey*, and *Foakes v. Beer* notwithstanding, the point could no longer be regarded as settled. To this, Peter Gibson L.J. (giving judgment on behalf of the Court) responded:

> I see the force of the argument, but the difficulty that I feel with it is that if the principle of *Williams'* case is to be extended to an obligation to make payment, it would in effect leave the principle in *Foakes v Beer* without any application. When a creditor and a debtor who are at arm's length reach agreement on the payment of the debt by instalments to accommodate the debtor, the creditor will no doubt always see a practical benefit to himself in so doing. In the absence of authority there would be much to be said for the enforceability of such a contract. But that was a matter expressly considered in *Foakes v Beer* yet held not to constitute good consideration in law. *Foakes v Beer* was not even referred to in *Williams'* case, and it is in my judgment impossible, consistently with the doctrine of precedent, for this Court to extend the principle of *Williams'* case to any circumstances governed by the principle of *Foakes v Beer*. If that extension is to be made, it must be by the House of Lords or, perhaps even more appropriately, by Parliament after consideration by the Law Commission.[33]

For the present, then, dynamic market-individualism must give way to the authority of precedent, leaving the law in a somewhat contradictory state (see Carter, Phang, and Poole, 1995). On the one hand, *Williams v Roffey* seems to cover (freely agreed but gratuitous) variations in favour of the creditor; yet, on the other hand, (freely agreed but gratuitous) variations in favour of the debtor remain covered by *Foakes v Beer* and the classical requirement of exchange.[34] One of the cornerstone features of static market-individualism thus retains a tenuous grip on the doctrine of consideration but, for the dynamic market-individualist, there is little doubt that the Court of Appeal in *Re Selectmove* must be seen as having missed an opportunity presented by *Williams v Roffey* to keep contract law closer in touch with commercial practice.

Implications

To appreciate the implications of the distinction between static and dynamic market-individualism, we need to consider how an awareness of doctrinal ideologies might contribute to our understanding of contract law.

Briefly, to return to our opening remarks, all legal doctrine is "ideological" in the sense that doctrine necessarily reflects particular ideas about how social life should be regulated. Accordingly, the first step towards understanding a particular branch of law (such as contract law) is to uncover the values that are presupposed by its leading doctrines. Identifying the ideological bearing of doctrine, however, is no mechanical operation; the process involves interpreting the doctrinal materials. Moreover, different interpretive methodologies prescribe different interpretive ground rules, each methodology having its own account of the "best interpretation" of the materials. For example, whilst one methodology might hold that the best interpretation is that which displays the smoothest fit between doctrine and ideology, or between segments of doctrine and particular ideologies, another methodology might hold that the best interpretation is that which relates doctrine to various independently-assured significant markers. For present purposes, we need say no more about these methodological complexities; it suffices to say that, whether we are concerned with "fit" alone or with some other criterion of interpretive power, there are grounds for thinking that the distinction between static and dynamic market-individualism will be material to our interpretive scheme.

Recall the two principal respects in which dynamic market-individualism departs from static market-individualism. First, the former takes a more flexible view of the situations in which contractual obligation may arise; and, secondly, it takes a potentially more restrictive view of the extent to which a contracting party may privilege its own economic interests. In both respects, however, dynamic market-individualism takes its lead from the commercial community—on the market side, it is as flexible as the relevant community allows and, on the individualistic side, it is as restrictive as that community requires. It follows that if "fit" is what we are looking for in an interpretive theory, we cannot get by with undifferentiated "market-individualism"; and if we are looking for something more than fit, the distinction between a form of market-individualism (static) that makes the market and one that largely tracks the market (dynamic) promises to be of some significance.

To pursue this last thought, it is tempting to see the significance of dynamic market-individualism in its recognition of the concept of legitimate expectation—indeed, not merely in its recognition of this concept, but in its placing of legitimate expectation at the core of its scheme of values. After all, within dynamic market-individualism, it is the expectations of the commercial community that determine where contractual obligation arises and where the line is to be drawn between permissible and impermissible transactional behaviour. It is possible, however, to present static market-individualism, too, as having a concern with legitimate expectation, in the sense that it is recognised that parties may form legitimate expectations on the basis of the declared (static) ground rules for contracting. Putting the matter this way, both static and dynamic market-individualism are concerned with the protection of legitimate expectations; but the difference is that the former treats the formal law as the exclusive source of such expectations while the latter treats the informal practice of the commercial community as the relevant source (the formal law simply reinforcing such expectations).

Even if the simple recognition of the concept of legitimate expectation is not directly the key to distinguishing between static and dynamic market-individualism, *the way in which this concept is implicated in the ideologies* highlights an important distinction for any interpretive theory. In principle, contract doctrine (and its accompanying ideology) might try to set a framework for (and channel) commercial practice or it might try merely to formalise practice. If we call an ideology of the former kind an independent contractual ideology and an ideology of the latter kind a dependent contractual ideology then, whereas static market-individualism is an independent contractual ideology, dynamic market-individualism is largely a dependent contractual ideology.

Now, one of the distinctive features of the dependent contractual ideology of dynamic market-individualism is that it allows for the commercial community to set its own standards of fairness and decency, to set its own restrictions on the pursuit of self-interest. Translated into legal doctrine, such restrictions are articulated as requirements of good faith. The constraining effect of good faith may be measured in two dimensions. The first dimension concerns the *scope* of the good faith requirement—in particular, is good faith required in negotiation as well as in the performance and enforcement of contracts, and is good faith required in all contractual dealings or only in those situations where the parties regularly deal with one another? The second dimension concerns the *depth* of good faith required. Here, the question is whether the doctrine of good faith amounts to no more than a restriction on the more obvious types of advantage-taking (e.g. as where it militates against seizing on the temporary vulnerability of one's fellow contractor to renegotiate the terms of the deal), or whether it actually requires acts of assistance (e.g. as where it requires disclosure of material facts during the negotiation or the performance of a contract) (cf. Collins, 1992). In other words, is good faith confined to a series of negative obligations or does it also place contracting parties under positive co-operative obligations? Although the answers to such questions tell us a good deal about the doctrine of good faith within a particular legal system and, concomitantly, about the commercial standards of that particular community, these are (dependent) variations within the broader framework of dynamic market-individualist thinking.

As the doctrinal landmarks associated with static market-individualism are gradually eroded (the doctrine of precedent notwithstanding), we can expect the tides of dynamic market-individualism to run ever more strongly. Does it follow, therefore, that dynamic market-individualism is set to become the ruling ideology of contract? Again, to return to our opening remarks, the general law of contract in the present century has been dominated by two ideologies, market-individualism and consumer-welfarism. The consumer side of consumer-welfarism does not, however, present any serious opposition to the rise of dynamic market-individualism; for the law of consumer contracts must be seen nowadays as a regulatory regime in its own right, severable for the most part from the general law of contract; and the welfarist side of consumer-welfarism is under-developed in its application to commercial contracting (see Brownsword, 1994b). It should not be thought, however, that the rise of dynamic market-individualism might occur, so to speak, faute de mieux. On the contrary, the shift to dynamic market-individualism (in conjunction with the severability of the law of consumer contracts) is very much in line with modern moral scepticism (cf. Scanlon, 1992), which translates into a concern that legal doctrine should at least be "acceptable" without necessarily being underwritten by any detached theory that renders it legitimate in a free-standing sense (cf. Teubner, 1983; Habermas, 1988; Brownsword, 1995). It follows that if there is to be a ruling ideology on the commercial wing of contract law, dynamic market-individualism is quite plainly the leading contender to emerge from the modern period.

The rise of dynamic market-individualism and the (relative) decline of its static counterpart should caution us, however, against assuming that the ideologies of contract are written in the skies. The ideologies of contract are subject to the ebb and flow of contemporary beliefs, values and attitudes (cf. Atiyah, 1978, 1979); and, already, contract theorists are speculating about the shape of the "post-modern" law of contract (see, e.g., Wilhelmsson, 1993, 1995). In the present context, this invites speculation about what might lie beyond dynamic market-individualism—possibly, a reaction against the uncertainties of commercial practice and opinion and a return to a detached ideology of some kind (whether based on the classical model of self-interested exchange or the modern model of co-operative relationships); or, perhaps, the elaboration of the welfarist ideal as a co-operative model of contract law. This, however, is an invitation to be accepted on another occasion, rather than at this late stage of the chapter. For the purposes of the present discussion, we can conclude on a less speculative note: the commercial law of contract is working its way free of the mould set by static market-individualism to become a regulatory regime dictated to a considerable extent by the informal expectations embedded in commercial practice and opinion—in other words, the emerging regime is inspired by a dynamic market-individualist approach. Accordingly, if we want to observe the cutting edge of contract law, then in the near future it is the ideology of dynamic market-individualism that should serve to focus our inquiries.

Notes

1. *New Zealand Shipping Co. Ltd. v. A.M. Satterthwaite and Co. Ltd.: The Eurymedon* [1975] A.C. 154.
2. At p. 167.
3. [1993] 1 Lloyd's L.R. 25.
4. Ibid., at p. 29.
5. (1992) 26 N.S.W.L.R. 234.
6. At p. 268, emphasis supplied.
7. *North Ocean Shipping Co. v. Hyundai Construction Co.: The Atlantic Baron* [1979] Q.B. 705.
8. [1990] 3 All E.R. 25.
9. [1990] 1 All E.R. 512.

10. [1990] 3 All E.R. 25, 30.
11. Ibid.
12. The standard examples of protecting pre-contractual reliance are *Hoffman v. Red Owl Stores* 26 Wis. 2d. 683 (1965) and *Walton's Stores (Interstate) Ltd. v. Maher* (1988) 76 A.L.R. 513. See, too, the important Canadian Supreme Court decision in *The Queen in Right of Ontario et al v. Ron Engineering and Construction Eastern Ltd.* 119 D.L.R. (3d) (1981) 267.
13. See, too, *Anangel Atlas Compania Naviera SA v. Ishikawajima-Harima Heavy Industries Co. Ltd. (No. 2)* [1990] 2 Lloyd's Rep. 526.
14. *KH Enterprise (cargo owners) v. Pioneer Container (owners): The Pioneer Container* [1994] 2 All E.R. 250, 255-6.
15. [1995] 1 All E.R. 691, 705.
16. [1995] 1 W.L.R. 68.
17. Ibid., at p. 76.
18. [1993] 3 All E.R. 417.
19. See Lord Diplock in *Albacruz (cargo owners) v. Albazero (owners): The Albazero* [1977] A.C. 774, 846-7.
20. [1995] 1 W.L.R. 68, 79.
21. *Philips Electronique Grand Public SA v. British Sky Broadcasting Ltd.; Philips International BV v. British Satellite Broadcasting Ltd* (unreported, 19 October, 1994).
22. Ibid.
23. Ibid.
24. [1992] 1 All E.R. 453.
25. [1995] 1 All E.R. 1005.
26. [1995] 2 All E.R. 531.
27. [1992] 1 All E.R. 453, 460-1.
28. Cf. *Coal Cliff Collieries Property Ltd. v Sijehama Property Ltd* (1991) 24 N.S.W.L.R. 1, and *Queensland Electricity Generating Board v New Hope Collieries Pty Ltd* [1989] 1 Lloyd's Rep. 205. For discussion of the latter in contrast to *Walford v Miles*, see McKendrick (1995, pp. 317-21)
29. [1977] 2 N.S.W.L.R. 880, esp. at 900-3.
30. [1995] 1 All E.R. 1005, 1024.
31. per Rattee J, ibid.
32. (1884) 9 App. Cas. 605.
33. [1995] 2 All E.R. 531, 538.
34. See, too, *Re C (A Debtor)* (C.A., May 11, 1994), discussed in Carter, Phang, and Poole (1995, pp 257-8).

Bibliography

Adams, John, and Brownsword, Roger (1987): "The Ideologies of Contract" 7 *Legal Studies* 207.

Adams, John, and Brownsword, Roger (1990a): "Contract, Consideration and the Critical Path" 53 *Modern Law Review* 536.

Adams, John, and Brownsword, Roger (1990b): "Privity and the Concept of a Network Contract" 10 *Legal Studies* 12.

Adams, John, and Brownsword, Roger (1992): *Understanding Law* (Fontana, London).

Adams, John, and Brownsword, Roger (1993): "Privity of Contract—That Pestilential Nuisance" 56 *Modern Law Review* 722.

Adams, John, and Brownsword, Roger (1994): *Understanding Contract Law* 2nd ed. (Fontana, London).

Adams, John, and Brownsword, Roger (1995): *Key Issues in Contract* (Butterworths, London).

Atiyah, Patrick S. (1978): *From Principles to Pragmatism* (Clarendon Press, Oxford).

Atiyah, Patrick S. (1979): *The Rise and Fall of Freedom of Contract* (Oxford University Press, Oxford).

Brownsword, Roger (1992): "Retrieving Reasons, Retrieving Rationality? A New Look at the Right to Withdraw for Breach of Contract" 5 *Journal of Contract Law* 83.

Brownsword, Roger (1993): "Towards a Rational Law of Contract" in Thomas Wilhelmsson (ed.) *Perspectives of Critical Contract Law* (Dartmouth Publishing Company, Aldershot) 241.

Brownsword, Roger (1994a): "Two Concepts of Good Faith" 7 *Journal of Contract Law* 197.

Brownsword, Roger (1994b): "The Philosophy of Welfarism and its Emergence in the Modern English Law of Contract" in Roger Brownsword, Geraint Howells and Thomas Wilhelmsson (eds) *Welfarism in Contract Law* (Dartmouth Publishing Company, Aldershot) 21.

Brownsword, Roger (1995): "The Limits of Freedom of Contract and the Limits of Contract Theory" 22 *Journal of Law and Society* 259.

Buckley, R.P. (1993): "*Walford v Miles*: False Certainty About Uncertainty—An Australian Perspective" 6 *Journal of Contract Law* 58.

Burton, Steven J. (1980-81): "Breach of Contract and the Common Law Duty to Perform in Good Faith" 94 *Harvard Law Review* 369.

Carter, J.W., Phang, Andrew and Poole, Jill (1995): "Reactions to *Williams v. Roffey*" 8 *Journal of Contract Law* 248.

Chen-Wishart, Mindy (1995): "Consideration: Practical Benefit and the Emperor's New Clothes" in Jack Beatson and Daniel Freedman (eds) *Good Faith and Fault in Contract Law* (Clarendon Press, Oxford) 123.

Cohen, Nili (1995): "Pre-Contractual Duties: Two Freedoms and the Contract to Negotiate" in Jack Beatson and Daniel Freedman (eds) *Good Faith and Fault in Contract Law* (Clarendon Press, Oxford) 25.

Collins, Hugh (1992): "Implied Duty to Give Information During Performance of Contracts" 55 *Modern Law Review* 556.

Daintith, Terence (1993): "Comment on Lewis: Markets, Regulation and Citizenship" in Roger Brownsword (ed.) *Law and the Public Interest* (Franz Steiner, Stuttgart) 139.

Eisenberg, Melvin A (1981-82): "The Bargain Principle and its Limits" 95 *Harvard Law Review* 741.

Eisenberg, Melvin A. (1995): "Relational Contracts" in Jack Beatson and Daniel Freedman (eds) *Good Faith and Fault in Contract Law* (Clarendon Press, Oxford) 291.

Farnsworth, E. Allan (1962-63): "Good Faith Performance and Commercial Reasonableness Under the Uniform Commercial Code" 30 *University of Chicago Law Review* 666.

Fredman, Sandra (1992): "The New Rights: Labour Law and Ideology in the Thatcher Years" 12 *Oxford Journal of Legal Studies* 24.

Galanter, Marc and Rogers, Joel (1988): "The Transformation of American Business Disputing? Some Preliminary Observations" paper presented at the Annual Meeting of the Law and Society Association, Colorado).

Graham, Cosmo and Prosser, Tony (1987): "Privatising Nationalised Industries: Constitutional Issues and New Legal Techniques" 50 *Modern Law Review* 16.

Habermas, Jürgen (1988): *Law and Morality: The Tanner Lectures on Human Values VIII.*

Harden, Ian J. (1992): *The Contracting State* (Open University Press, Milton Keynes).

Halson, Roger (1990): "Sailors, Sub-Contractors and Consideration" 106 *Law Quarterly Review* 183.

Kronman, A (1980): "Contract Law and Distributive Justice" 89 *Yale Law Journal* 472.

Law Commission (1991): *Privity of Contract: Contracts for the Benefit of Third Parties* (Consultation Paper No. 121).

McKendrick, Ewan (1995): "The Regulation of Long-Term Contracts in English Law" in Jack Beatson and Daniel Freedman (eds) *Good Faith and Fault in Contract Law* (Clarendon Press, Oxford) 305.

Scanlon, T. M. (1992): "The Aims and Authority of Moral Theory" 12 *Oxford Journal of Legal Studies* 1.

Teubner, Gunther (1983): "Substantive and Reflexive Elements in Modern Law" 17 *Law and Society Review* 239.

Vincent-Jones, Peter (1993): "Contract Litigation in England and Wales 1975-91: A Transformation in Business Disputing?" *Civil Justice Quarterly* 337.

Wilhelmsson, Thomas (1993): "Questions for a Critical Contract Law—and a Contradictory Answer: Contract as Social Cooperation" in Thomas

Wilhelmsson (ed.) *Perspectives of Critical Contract Law* (Dartmouth Publishing Company, Aldershot) 9.

Wilhelmsson, Thomas (1995): *Social Contract Law and European Integration* (Dartmouth Publishing Company, Aldershot).

4 Contracting in the Haven: Balfour v. Balfour Revisited

MICHAEL FREEMAN

> *Balfour* v *Balfour* is one of those wise decisions in which the courts allow the realities of life to determine the legal norm which they formulate (Otto Kahn-Freund[1]).

Balfour v *Balfour,*[2] three quarters of a century after it was decided, remains a leading case. It features prominently in all contract textbooks and, as Treitel observes,[3] it has not been judicially questioned. It has had one in-depth critical article devoted to it but this, by Stephen Healey,[4] concentrates mainly on the place of the case in the law of contract.

My starting point is somewhat different. As a family lawyer I am struck by a paradox. The ruling orthodoxy remains *Balfour* v *Balfour* but increasingly English law extends to those in family relationships the power to regulate their own lives. Nor is English law alone in exemplifying this trend.[5] Oddly, as commercial law has come to learn the perils of an uncritical embrace of freedom of contract as its governing principle,[6] so family law, for so long its paradigmatic antithesis, has welcomed the ideological framework of contract. As contract law has shifted its direction towards status,[7] as it has come to reflect ongoing relationships[8] with reliance[9] rather than choice its key, so modern family law has steadily embraced contract as its governing principle and in the process has cast off many of its status associations.[10] Once no clearer antimony was drawn than that which separated the family and the market.[11] The family was quintessentially "private": commerce, by contrast, belonged to the "public" world.[12] But the family, that "haven from the heartless world"[13] of the market has now adopted many of the same concepts and principles that (once) commerce embraced.

And yet *Balfour* v *Balfour* remains ruling orthodoxy. The standard examples still given in contract textbooks of agreements or arrangements where there is no intention to create a legal relationship, and therefore no contract, are those in family relationships, in particular between husbands and wives.[14]

Not only has family law changed since *Balfour* v *Balfour*, but there have also been enormous changes in the way people regulate their domestic arrangements. When *Balfour* v *Balfour* was decided in 1921 what we would understand today as cohabitation was unheard of. Men had mistresses - this is evident from another leading contract case of the period *Upfill* v *Wright*[15] - but the phenomenon of cohabitation outside marriage[16] was discretely veiled. It was the 1970s, fifty years after *Balfour* v *Balfour*, before the courts began to confront the problems caused by dysfunctional cohabitation arrangements.[17]

Does *Balfour* v *Balfour* accordingly have much relevance today? Does it remain a "wise" decision in tune with the realities of life? Was such an astute observer as Otto Kahn-Freund, a founding father of academic family law in this country,[18] wrong or have our perceptions of wisdom changed in the forty-three years since his remarks appeared in the *Modern Law Review*? It is my view that there is now a mismatch between the so-called governing principle and the realities of family life. Indeed, that family law itself, as it has come to embrace contract, has ignored, and wisely so, the ruling orthodoxy of contract lawyers. Before this argument can proceed, *Balfour* v *Balfour* itself needs to be critically examined.

Balfour v *Balfour*

The facts of *Balfour* v *Balfour* could not be more straightforward. The parties were married in 1900. The husband, a civil engineer, had a post with the government of Ceylon as Director of Irrigation. At the end of a period of leave spent in England in 1916, the wife, who suffered from rheumatic arthritis, stayed on in England on medical advice. The husband promised to pay his wife £30 a month during the period of their separation whilst he was in Ceylon. Some eighteen months later he wrote suggesting that they had better remain apart. She sought and was granted a decree of restitution of conjugal rights, and an order for alimony. The law report does not disclose the amount of this award but we may assume it was probably quite small.[19] The wife also sued on the promise of maintenance, presumably, though it is not clear from the report, to supplement her alimony award. If there were any conflict of laws issues in the case, they were not raised.[20] We may, however, assume that Mr Balfour's domicile remained English.

Sargant J. decided in Mrs Balfour's favour:[21] he found consideration for the contract in her forbearance from seeking to pledge his credit for necessaries.[22] The Court of Appeal allowed Mr Balfour's appeal.[23] The three judgments do not pursue identical lines of argument and Atkin L.J.'s is, perhaps not surprisingly, the most interesting.

Whilst Warrington L.J. and Duke L.J. might have been prepared to dispose of Mrs Balfour's action because of the absence, as they saw it, of consideration, it is Atkin L.J. who, with a flourish of language and an eye on theory, articulates what has become the orthodox legal argument. He lays down, what Unger called,[24] the "charmed circle" of family arrangements. "In respect of these promises", Atkin L.J. says, "each house is a domain into which the King's wait does not seek to run, and to which his officers do not seek to be admitted".[25] There could not be a clearer statement of the privacy argument, to which I will return.

Atkin L.J. continued that, even if there were consideration, arrangements such as that entered into by the Balfours "are not contracts, and they are not contracts because the parties did not intend that they should be attended by legal consequences".[26] In Atkin L.J.'s opinion, "agreements such as these are outside the realm of contracts altogether".[27] It should be noted that the privacy argument has thus been supplemented by an altogether different one, namely that parties in domestic situations do not intend to be contractually bound. Subtle distinctions between subjective intention and objective intention do not appear to have concerned Atkin L.J., though it would seem that he is imputing intention on the basis of what might be expected from persons in the situation of the Balfours. But note he does not put this into any reasonable spouses' context. People in the position of the Balfours do not intend to be contractually bound because judges do not want them to come under the umbrella of contract protection.

Atkin L.J. uses, it should be noted, two common reasoning techniques: *reductio ad absurdum* and the slippery slope argument. Thus, he starts his judgment by invoking the social arrangement ("Two parties agree to take a walk together or ... there is an offer and acceptance of hospitality").[28] This leads him straight into the conclusion that agreements between husbands and wives, many of which are of course of this kind but some of which are, as in *Balfour* v *Balfour* itself, on matters of real importance, should be treated similarly.

He also reasons, using the well-known floodgates argument, that if the court were to conclude there were a contract between the Balfours "the small Courts of this country would have to be multiplied one hundredfold".[29] Duke L.J. agreed. He foresaw "unlimited litigation in a relationship which should be obviously as far as possible protected from possibilities of that kind".[30] Such fears are entirely exaggerated, even more so in 1921 when there was no legal aid. Warrington L.J.'s judgment employs the *reductio ad absurdum* argument too - indeed, he admits as much. "If", he argues, "we were to hold that there was a contract in this case we should have to hold that with regard to all the more or less trivial concerns of life where a wife, at the request of her husband, makes a promise to him, that is a promise which can be enforced in law".[31] At most, in Warrington L.J.'s view, the husband was "bound in honour"[32] to pay the sum he had promised: the wife, however, in his view, "made no bargain at all".[33] The *reductio ad absurdum* reasoning, particularly as it features in Warrington L.J.'s judgment, is weak: it is easily arguable that with trivial matters there is no intention to create legal relations. An agreement about support - in issue in *Balfour* v *Balfour* - comes into a very different category. But this assumes that Warrington L.J. saw the case as about intention to create legal relations, and that may be doubted.

The textbook writers, Leake,[34] Pollock,[35] Anson,[36] wrote of the need for there to be an intention to create legal relations long before *Balfour* v *Balfour*. It is true others did not (Chitty only recognises the requirement in 1930, 102 years after his first edition and nine after *Balfour* v *Balfour),*[37] but it seems to be the case that academic doctrine antedates precedent in this area. It is inconceivable that Atkin L.J. will not have read Pollock or Anson, though he does not refer to them. If he were aware that he was propounding a novel proposition, with support only in academic textbooks, we might have expected him to cite them in support. They were long dead, so that the absurd obstacle of not citing living authors would not have obtruded.[38]

After *Balfour* v *Balfour* the textbook writers were able to seize upon the case, and in particular Atkin L.J.'s judgment, to clothe with authority what they had previously based on principle or civilian writings like Pothier and Savigny.[39] Atkin L.J.'s judgment came to be seen as judicial support for the intention to create legal relations requirement. Pre-*Balfour* it was easy to conceptualise this in terms of the absence of consideration, and this is thinking still firmly rooted in the judgments of Duke L.J. and Warrington L.J. It was some years after before Atkin L.J.'s judgment attracted attention. Indeed, only in the 1940s did the requirement of an "intention to create legal relations" achieve prominence in the case law.[40] It is difficult to explain why, but it seems - we can, of course, rely on reported cases only - that not until this time did plaintiffs seek to apply contract outside its normal commercial context. Or, perhaps, only then did defendants resist attempts to do so.

It must not be forgotten that *Balfour* v *Balfour* was decided only a generation after married women acquired the capacity to make contracts with their husbands:[41] another fourteen years were to elapse before they acquired complete contractual capacity.[42] The social changes since 1919 have been enormous. The doctrine enunciated in *Balfour* v *Balfour* lives on. The cases provide several instances of its application. One of the more significant is *Gould* v *Gould*.[43] The majority in this case (Edmund Davies and Megaw L.J.J.) did not think that the form of words used by a working class husband in saying that he would pay his wife £15 a week "so long as he had it" imported sufficient certainty as to indicate that the parties intended to enter into legal relations. The agreement in issue had been entered into after the husband and wife separated. An equally valid conclusion is that the parties had intended a contractually-binding arrangement but lacked the ability to formulate this agreement in language acceptable to the Court of Appeal.

Lord Denning M.R.'s dissenting judgment is the more interesting of the judgments in *Gould* v *Gould*. He conceded that "the question of an "intent to create legal relations" [was] not to be resolved by looking into the minds of the parties". By contrast, "it is not the actual intention of the parties, but the intention that the court imputes to them. It is to be found by looking at what the parties said and did in the situation in which they found themselves: and then asking: what would reasonable people think about the provision? Would they regard it as intended to be binding? If it was a firm promise, made for good consideration, a reasonable person will, as a rule, have regarded it as intended to be binding: and the courts will enforce it unless it was a mere domestic or social arrangement".[44] It is a fair suspicion that reasonable people, certainly people who understood the lives of couples like the Goulds, would have concluded that they had made a binding agreement. They may also have found sufficient certainty in the agreement. Should we expect agreements such as those entered into by the Balfours and the Goulds, and entered into orally, to look like formal contracts found in the business world?

The facts of *Gould* v *Gould* were different from those in *Balfour* v *Balfour*. In the earlier case, the agreement was entered into in a state of amity (or so we must assume): in the latter case, the parties had already separated.[45] Mrs Balfour lost her case because she could not prove that there was a contract - she was arguably the first litigant to have to prove this. Mrs Gould lost her case because the agreement was not sufficiently commercial enough - it was not formulised in sufficiently precise language.

How to deny contractual remedies

From the cases considered and from others we can find at least three processes of reasoning used by the judges to conclude that arrangements between husbands and wives - and we will see between cohabitants - should be denied contractual remedies. The three arguments adduced are not necessarily consistent, nor is there any necessary coherence between them. This is the world of "mix and match", rather than of scientific exposition.

The first argument is that the presumption against finding a contract accords with the parties' intentions. This argument emphasises private autonomy: the parties do not want their agreement to have legal consequences and it would accordingly be wrong for a court to gainsay their decision.

But public-regarding arguments are also found. The first of these suggests that intimate relationships are too private for court intervention through contract enforcement to be appropriate. The intuitive appeal of this is obvious, until it is realised that all contractual relationships are private. The law of contract, whatever its juridical basis, is there to facilitate and enforce private arrangements. A ready, if unconvincing, response to this is that business arrangements, whilst private, are not as private as intimate arrangements. But there are different sorts of intimate arrangements too. The differentiation suggested here becomes all the more unsatisfactory when we look at the relationship of cohabitation outside marriage, an area where the courts have had to grapple with domestic arrangements constantly in the last 20 years.

Balfour v *Balfour* long ante-dates the renewed trend towards living together as husband and wife outside marriage. However, if we look at a case decided eight years before *Balfour*, we are confronted, albeit inchoately, with a further public argument.

The case of *Upfill* v *Wright*[46] concerned not a cohabitation agreement as such but a tenancy agreement where the landlord knew that the tenant's rent would be paid by her lover. The court could not distinguish the tenant's situation from that of a prostitute and, following *Pearce* v *Brooks*,[47] held that, since the flat was let for an immoral purpose - the court had no doubt that "fornication", as it called it, was immoral - the landlord could not recover rent which was owed. The court was not interested in intention. Nor was it concerned that the stigmatized relationship was an intimate one. What led the court to conclude that the tenancy agreement could not be enforced were the very public considerations of public policy. The court saw itself as the guardian of public morality. Its role was conceived as being to reinforce public standards and to condemn deviant relationships. In *Walker* v *Perkins*[47.a] and *Benyon* v *Nettlefold*,[48] much earlier cases, this public policy role is forcefully maintained. In 1938 Lord Wright in *Fender* v *St. John Mildmay* expressed the same view in the clearest of terms. It was his view that "the law will not enforce an immoral purpose, such as a promise between a man and a woman to live together without being married or to pay a sum of money or to give some other consideration in return for an immoral consideration".[49] This, as Cretney[50] writing in 1974 noted, was still thought to represent English law - and probably remains orthodox doctrine even today. This tends to be forgotten largely, I suspect, because the very many cases that have been litigated in the last twenty years the contract has either been at arm's length after separation,[51] or the very absence of a contract has forced the courts to fall back on the law of trusts[52] where, curiously, these considerations of public policy do not seem to obtrude. Yet, in these cases it is the absence of an agreement[53] which compels the courts to seek justice in the law of trusts and allows them conveniently to pass over whatever is left of the public policy considerations.

The arguments appraised

The three lines of reasoning do not convince. Of the three the public policy rationale can be most readily disposed of. If public policy is to reflect public rather than judicial opinion it clearly has no place in the changed social environment of today.[54]

The privacy argument must be recognised for what it is. The law has long claimed to be absent in the "private" world of family and domestic life.[55] Thus, it was not until 1962 that husbands and wives could sue each other in tort[56]. Rape in marriage only became criminal with *R* v *R* in 1991.[57] The marital rape immunity remarkably was justified by implying a term into the marriage contract (the terms of which were fixed by common law, not the parties)[58] that most women in the last fifty years at least would have rejected.[59] Wife beating was initially omitted from the definition of criminal assault on the ground that the husband had the right to chastise his wife.[60] Subsequently, police reluctance to intervene in wife battering was justified on privacy grounds.[61] The rhetoric of privacy has insulated the female world from the legal order and, in doing so, has sent an important ideological message to society. It devalues women by saying that they are not important enough to merit legal regulation. Taub and Schneider argue that

> This message is clearly communicated when particular relief is withheld. By declining to punish a man for inflicting injuries on his wife, for example, the law implies she is his property and he is free to control her as he sees fit. Women's work is discredited when the law refuses to enforce the man's obligation to support his wife, since it implies she makes no contribution worthy of support. Similarly, when courts decline to enforce contracts that seek to limit or specify the extent of the wife's services, the law implies that household work is not real work in the way that the type of work subject to contract in the public sphere is real work. These are important messages, for denying woman's humanity and the value of her traditional work are key ideological components in maintaining woman's subordinate status. The message of women's inferiority is compounded by the totality of the law's absence from the private realm. In our society law is for business and other important things.[62]

Nor should it be forgotten that what we protect as "private" is a political decision and this has important "public" consequences,[63] or that failures to respond, whether it be to domestic violence or to claims to enforce a contract, are public, not private, actions.[64]

What is constantly overlooked is the inconsistency between the privacy argument, which says that what goes on in intimate relationships is no business of the state, and the public policy argument which, for example, does not allow parties who wish to do so to deviate from the standard terms of a marriage contract. Why are the parties not free to vary the terms of their relationship without interference by the state? Thus, to take one example, the law says that a marriage contract is incomplete without sexual intercourse taking place.[65] Accordingly, an agreement before marriage not to have sexual intercourse after its celebration is said to strike fundamentally at the basis of the marriage itself,[66] in the same manner as is an agreement entered into before marriage for a future separation.[67]

The intention argument is also far from unproblematic. Contracts between husbands and wives will often be oral rather than written. The courts, despite the

74

emphasis on what the parties intended, are wary of subjective intention and seem to look both to context and to formal criteria. There is a tendency to emphasise factors external to the parties and their actual intentions (in so far as these can be gleaned). But in doing this the courts are applying the same techniques as they would in a trusts or restitution case. In effect whether they find an agreement ultimately rests on public-sounding considerations. Clare Dalton,[68] writing of cohabitation agreements in the United States, has observed that different judges can interpret virtually identical agreements differently: she explains this in terms of "their views of what policy should prevail or their own moral sense".[69]

Contract and family law: a mismatch

The Balfours was a Victorian marriage. The ideals of Victorian marriages and values concerning the family lasted until perhaps a generation ago.[70] But where the emphasis was on status, it is now on autonomy. For role identification we have now substituted role distance.[71] The "self" and individual choice have replaced role and obligation as central organising concepts. Whether this is a good or a bad thing is outside the remit of this article: certainly, communitarianism has become attractive to those who find the individualism embraced by the new model destructive of the good society.[72]

Modern family law, responding to this trend, has embraced contract as its governing principle. Despite the ruling orthodoxy of *Balfour* v *Balfour*, private ordering, rather than public regulation, has become the preferred means of organising and governing relationships within the family.[73] I speak of trends - in the coda of an article nominally addressing contract rather than family law issues I can do no more[74] - and there are clear and important exceptions to dominant trends. Thus, for example, the broad equitable redistributive powers of a court upon divorce[75] and the paramountcy principle that has come to govern the Solomonic decision[76] where a child's living arrangements are disputed[77] do not fit the trend depicted here.

This trend, as one American observer has put it, "has evolved far toward recognizing the need for private choice and the untenableness of uniform public policy as a strategy for governing the conduct and obligations of intimacy".[78]

Thus, entry into marriage is less regulated than it was and is more dependent upon individual choice.[79] The law relating to affinity was relaxed in 1986,[80] that relating to capacity to enter into a polygamous marriage has been liberalised by both case law[81] and also by recent legislation.[82] The places where marriages can be celebrated now takes greater account of what the parties want.[83] It is unlikely that you will ever be able to choose to marry a close blood relation, though there have been calls to allow brothers and sisters to marry,[84] but, it may be expected that some relaxation will take place in time (perhaps allowing uncles and nieces and aunts and nephews to marry).[85] It is inevitable that the law will come to allow people to choose their own sex, in that the bar on transsexuals marrying is likely to revoked.[86] Similarly, it can only be a matter of time before we allow, as the three Scandinavian countries already do, the registration of gay partnerships.[87]

The law is also more willing to let those who are married define the terms of their relationship. Husbands and wives can sue each other, in contract[88] and in tort.[89] And, although a spouse cannot by his or her own covenant preclude him or herself from invoking the jurisdiction of the court or preclude the court from the exercise of that jurisdiction,[90] courts nevertheless start from the position that a solemn and freely-negotiated bargain by which a party with competent legal advice defines his or her own requirements ought to be adhered to unless some clear and compelling reason is shown to the contrary.[91] An agreement between spouses cannot fetter the jurisdiction of the court, but a court order which makes a once-and-for-all financial provision for a party to the marriage or dismisses that party's claim to financial relief operates as a bar to any fresh application for a court order.[92] This is the basis on which so called "clean break" orders[93] are routinely made by consent in matrimonial proceedings. One illustration may be given. In *Edgar* v *Edgar*,[94] the wife of a multi-millionaire entered into an agreement whereby she accepted property worth £100,000 from her husband and agreed not to seek any further capital or property provision from him whether by way of ancillary relief in divorce proceedings or otherwise. Three years later she petitioned for divorce, claimed a substantial sum and at first instance was indeed awarded a lump sum of £760,000. But the Court of Appeal held that she had shown insufficient grounds to justify going behind the original agreement. The court conceded that the husband had not exploited this in a way which was unfair to the wife. She had had the benefit of proper professional advice and had deliberately chosen to ignore it.[95]

It may be thought that this emphasis on private ordering is not inconsistent with the *Balfour* principle. But this can only be so on the basis that courts, so it is said, are prepared to impute to husbands and wives an intention to create legal relations where they decide to separate and make an agreement to govern their future financial relationship.[96] But, again, it needs to be stressed that actual intentions are often ignored by the courts so that husbands and wives, it seems, will often be deemed by a court to have entered into a contract only in circumstances where it finds contract the appropriate mechanism to describe the relationship. Private ordering is then permitted for public-regarding reasons.

In addition to greater control over entry into marriage and its terms, husbands and wives have been given greater powers to determine for themselves when to leave the marital relationship. The shift to no-fault divorce,[97] which will be completed when the latest proposals[98] are implemented very soon, reflects a conception of marriage as a private matter, controlled by the preferences of the parties. The U.S. Supreme Court has come close to articulating a right to divorce.[99] The White Paper, *Looking to the Future*, envisages, although it does not explicitly formulate as much, the termination of marriage (albeit after a period of "reflection") on the "say-so" of one party. We have got beyond talk of divorce upon mutual agreement to an acceptance of repudiation. In a country where there is no society only individuals,[100] the social bond of marriage cannot count for much. It is at least arguable that Muslim women in Pakistan, for example, will get greater protection from the *talaq* than English women will get from the Lord Chancellor's divorce proposals.[101]

The conceptualization of marriage as a private matter is emphasised also by the trend to define marital fault very narrowly in property and money determinations[102] and in disputes about children.[103] This reflects, what Regan calls, "agnosticism about marital behavior".[104] And he notes a link between this and no-fault divorce: "if the state feels less able to assess the propriety of behavior in an existing marriage, then it is in a poor position to proclaim what behavior justifies ending the marriage".[105] Clean break policies, the preference for lump sums rather than periodical payments and time limits on alimony also reflect policy decisions to allow the individual to move on unencumbered by past choices.

Conclusion

Marriage has become "a personal rather than a social institution",[106] fit for private ordering rather than state regulation. And yet the official version of the truth is that husbands and wives do not subject their arrangements to the law of contract. If *Balfour* v *Balfour* was a "wise" decision based on the "realities" of life, then wisdom dictates that we rethink the doctrine it embodies. It no longer reflects realities nor is it in line with developments taking place in family law. Once the fiction is rejected we will be in a position to assess the role of contract in intimate relationships and to examine the relevance of the modern law of contract on the family.

Notes

1. "Inconsistencies and Injustices in the Law of Husband and Wife", [1952] 15 *Modern Law Review* 133, 138.
2. [1919] 2 K.B. 571.
3. *The Law of Contract* (London: Sweet and Maxwell, 9th ed., 1995), p. 152. Though its facts are said to stretch the doctrine to its limits: *Pettit* v *Pettit* [1970] A.C. 806, 816.
4. "Keeping Contract in its Place - *Balfour* v *Balfour* and the Enforceability of Informal Agreements", [1985] 5 *Oxford Journal of Legal Studies* 391.
5. "Keeping contract in its Place - *Balfour* v *Balfour* and the Enforceability of Informal Agreements", [1985] 5 *Oxford Journal of Legal Studies* 391.

6. See Patrick Atiyah, *The Rise and Fall of Freedom of Contract* (Oxford: Clarendon Press, 1979).

7. See Slawson, "The New Meaning of Contract: the Transformation of Contract Law by Standard Terms" [1984] 46 *University of Pittsburgh Law Review* 21.

8. See the work of Stewart Macaulay (*Law and the Balance of Powers* [1966]) and "Elegant Models, Empirical Pictures and the Complexities of Contract" [1977] 11 *Law and Society Review* 507, as well as the early study "Non-Contractual Relations in Business: A Preliminary Study" [1963] 28 *American Sociological Review* 55.·

9. See Atiyah, op. cit., note 6 and his *Promises, Morals and the Law* (Oxford: Clarendon Press, 1974). See also G. Gilmore, *The Death of Contract* (Columbus: Ohio State University, 1974). But cf. C. Fried, *Contract As Promise* (Cambridge, Mass.: Harvard University Press, 1981) (where contract is justified as an enforcement of promises).

10. See K. O'Donovan, *Family Law Matters* (London: Pluto Press, 1993).

11. See M.D.A. Freeman, "Towards a Critical Theory of Family Law" [1985] 38 *Current Legal Problems* 153.

12. See James Gordley, *The Philosophical Origins of Modern Contract Doctrine* (Oxford: Clarendon Press, 1991).

13. In Christopher Lasch's well-known expression: see his book *Haven in a Heartless World* (New York: Basic Books, 1977).

14. Though not exclusively: see, for example, *Jones* v *Padavatton* [1969] 1 W.L.R. 328.

15. [1911] 1 K.B. 506.

16. On which see Michael Freeman and Christina Lyon, *Cohabitation without Marriage* (Aldershot: Gower, 1983).

17. *Diwell* v *Farnes* [1959] 1 W.L.R. 624, 631 *per* Ormerod L.J.

18. His course at L.S.E. in the 1940s was probably the first academic course in the country. In a lecture reminiscing on this he tells of walking through the Temple and astonishing a divorce barrister by telling him that family law included the law of marriage as well as divorce.

19. Such awards were very small until quite recently.

20. It must be presumed that the putative proper law of this contract was English law.

21. [1919] 35 T.L.R. 476.

22. As she could have done then. This was not abolished until 1970.

23. [1919] 2 K.B. 571.

24. "Intent to Create Legal Relations, Mutuality and Consideration", [1985] 19 *Modern Law Review* 96, 98. But cf. Hugh Collins, *The Law of Contract* (London: Butterworths, 2nd ed. 1993), p. 90 where the absence of consideration is seen as at the root of *Balfour* v *Balfour*.

25. Op. cit., note 2, p. 579.

26. Idem.

27. Idem.
28. Ibid., p. 578.
29. Ibid., p. 579.
30. Ibid., p. 577.
31. Ibid., p. 575.
32. Idem.
33. Idem.
34. *The Elements of the Law of Contracts* (1st ed., 1867), p. 9.
35. *Principles of the English Law Contract* (1st ed., 1876), p. 2.
36. *Principles of Contract: Being a Treatise on the General Principles Concerning the Validity of Agreements to the Law of England* (1st ed., 1879), p. 14.
37. Only in his 1st edition, edited by MacFarlane and Wrangham in 1930 is the doctrine first mentioned.
38. According to Atiyah, op. cit., note 6, p. 690 "in 1919 Lord Atkin borrowed Pollock's ideas and gave them judicial support in *Balfour* v *Balfour*".
39. Leake used Pothier (but also Austin, Maine and the French *Code Civil*): Pollock relies on Savigny. On these influences see Gordley, op. cit., note 12.
40. *Peters* v *IRC* [1941] 2 All E.R. 620 (though *Balfour* v *Balfour* was not cited or referred to in the judgments).
41. In 1882 with the Married Women's Property Act. *Hall* v *Michelmore* [1901] 18 T.L.R. 33 seems to be the first case in which such a contract is alleged.
42. In 1935 with the Law Reform (Married Women and Tortfeasors) Act.
43. [1969] 3 All E.R. 728.
44. Ibid., p. 730.
45. And see *Merritt* v *Merritt* [1970] 1 W.L.R. 1121.
46. Op. cit., note 15. The case was viewed with some scepticism in *Heglibiston Establishment* v *Heyman* [1977] 36 P. and C.R. 351.
47. [1866] L.R. 1 Ex. 213.
47.a. [1764] 1 W.B. 517.
48. [1850] 3 Mac. and G. 94.
49. [1938] A.C. 1, 42.
50. *Principles of Family Law* (London: Sweet and Maxwell, 1974), p. 31.
51. For example, see *Ward* v *Byham* [1956] 2 All E.R. 318 and *Tanner* v *Tanner* [1975] 2 All E.R. 716.
52. *Pettitt* v *Pettitt* [1970] A.C. 777; *Gissing* v *Gissing* [1971] A.C. 886, cf. *Lloyds Bank* v *Rosset* [1991] 1 A.C. 107 and *Burns* v *Burns* [1984] Ch. 317.
53. See, for example, *Springette* v *Defoe* [1992] 2 F.L.R. 388.
54. In a quarter of a century cohabitation has been transformed from the practice of 6 per cent of couples before their wedding day to close on 60

per cent. See K. Kilruan and V. Estaugh, *Cohabitation: Extra-Marital Child Bearing and Social Policy* (London: Family Policies Centre, 1993).

55. See F. Olsen, "The Family and the Market: A study of Ideology and Legal Reform", [1983] 96 *Harvard Law Review* 1497.

56. Law Reform (Husband and Wife) Act 1962.

57. [1992] 1 A.C. 599.

58. See Lenore Weitzman, *The Marriage Contract* (New York: Free Press, 1981).

59. The reasoning is usually traced to Sir Matthew Hale's *Pleas of the Crown*. See Michael Freeman, "Doing His Best to Sustain the Sanctity of Marriage" in N. Johnson (ed.), *Marital Violence* (London: Routledge, 1985).

60. And See Mavis Doggett, *Marriage, Wife-beating and the Law in Victorian England* (London: Weidenfeld and Nicolson, 1992).

61. See M.D.A. Freeman, *Violence in the Home - a Socio-Legal Study* (Aldershot: Gower, 1979).

62.

"Perspectives on Women's Subordination and the Role of Law" in David Kairys (ed.), *The Politics of Law: A Progressive Critique* (New York: Pantheon, 1982), pp. 122-3.

63. See Frank Michelman, "Private, Personal but not Split: *Radin v Rorty*", [1990] 63 *Southern California Law Review* 1783, 1794.

64. See Martha Minow, "Words and the Door to the Land of Change: Law, Language and Family Violence", [1990] 45 *Vanderbilt Law Review* 1665, 1672.

65. See Richard Collier, *Masculinity, Law and the Family* (London: Routledge, 1995).

66. *Scott v Scott* (*orse Fone*) [1959] P. 103, 106 *per* Sachs J.

67. *Brodie v Brodie* [1917] P. 271; *Hudston v Hudston* [1922] 39 T.L.R. 108, 111 *per* Horridge J.

68. "An Essay in the Deconstruction of Contract", [1985] 94 *Yale Law Journal* 997.

69. Ibid., p. 1102.

70. On which see S. Mintz, *A Prison of Expectations: The Family in Victorian Culture* (1983). See also Michael Grossberg, *Governing the Hearth* (Chapel Hill: University of North Carolina Press, 1985).

71. See Milton Regan, *Family Law and the Pursuit of Intimacy* (New York: New York University Press, 1993) pp. 46-56. See also Robert Bellah et al., *Habits of the Heart* (Berkeley: University of California Press, 1985) and Charles Taylor, *Sources of the Self* (Cambridge, Mass.: Harvard University Press, 1989).

72. See Robert Bellah et al., *The Good Society* (New York: Knopf, 1991).

73. See Jana B. Singer, "The Privatization of Family Law" (1992) *Wisconsin Law Review* 1443.

74. See Mary-Ann Glendon, *The Transformation of Family Law* (Chicago: University of Chicago Press, 1989).

75. See Matrimonial Causes Act 1973 s. 25.

76. See Jon Elster, "Solomonic Judgments: Against the Best Interests of the Child", (1987) 54 *University of Chicago Law Review* 1.

77. See Children Act 1987 s. 1 (1) (and see the welfare checklist in s. 1 (3)).

78. See Marjorie M. Schultz, "Contractual Ordering of Marriage: A New Model for State Policy" (1982) 70 *California Law Review* 204, 291.

79. In the U.S. where formerly there were miscegenation statutes this is even more marked. See *Loving* v *Virginia* 388 U.S. 1 [1967]. Also of interest is *Turner* v *Safley* 482 U.S. 78 [1987] (ruling unconstitutional the requirement that prison inmates required the governor's permission to marry).

80. By the Marriage (Prohibited Degrees of Relationship) Act 1986.

81. *Radwan* v *Radwan (No. 2)* [1973] Fam. 37 and *Hussein* v *Hussein* [1983] Fam 26.

82. See the Private International Law (Miscellaneous Provisions) Act 1995, part II.

83. As a result of the Marriage Act 1994, though local authorities retain ultimate control and are unlikely to relax the law governing place of celebration unduly. My own local authority is ambivalent about weddings being celebrated in Wembley Stadium.

84. There have been well-publicised examples of cohabitation: in all these cases the brother and sister had not been brought up together. This weakens the social objections but not necessarily the eugenic considerations.

85. Cf. *Cheni* v *Cheni* [1965] P. 85 (marriage in Egypt between Jews domiciled in Egypt upheld in England and ruled not offensive to our standards of decency and Christian morality).

86. This ban was upheld in *Corbett* v *Corbett (orse Ashley)* [1971] P. 83 and subsequently by the European Court on Human Rights in *Cossey* v *U.K.* [1991] 2 F.L.R. 492 and *Rees* v *U.K. (No. 2)* [1987] 2 F.L.R. 111.

87. See Symposium, "The Family in the 1990s: And Exploration of Gay and Lesbian Rights", (1991) 1 *Law and Sexuality* 1.

88. See op. cit, note 41.

89. Since 1962: the court may stay the action where (in its view) no substantial benefit would accrue to either party.

90. *Hyman* v *Hyman* [1929] A.C. 601.

91. *Edgar* v *Edgar* [1980] 1 W.L.R. 1410.

92. *De Lasala* v *De Lasala* [1980] A.C. 546.

93. *Minton* v *Minton* [1979] A.C. 593.

94. [1980] 1 W.L.R. 1410.

95. See *Camm* v *Camm* [1982] 4 F.L.R. 577.

96. Cf. *Merritt* v *Merritt* [1970] 1 W.L.R. 1211. It is worth comparing the approaches of Lord Denning M.R. (at p. 1213) and Widgery L.J. (at p. 1214).

97. With the Divorce Reform Act 1969 (the sole ground for divorce being irretrievable breakdown, but adultery, behaviour and desertion retained as "facts").

98. *Looking to the Future: Mediation and the Ground of Divorce*, Cm. 2799 (London: H.M.S.O., 1995).

99. In *Boddie* v *Connecticut* 401 U.S. 371 (1971).

100. According to that well-known sociologist, Margaret Thatcher.

101. Although the Pakistan Muslim Family Law Ordinance of 1961 provides for a 90 day period (for conciliation) and the English law will provide a 12 month breathing space.

102. Conduct is taken into account only where it would be inequitable to disregard it (see Matrimonial Causes Act 1973 s. 25 (2) (g)).

103. See *S (BD)* v *S (DJ)* [1977] Fam. 109; *Re K* [1977] Fam. 179.

104. *Family Law and the Pursuit of Intimacy* (New York: New York University Press, 1993), p. 39.

105. Idem.

106. *Per* Temple, op. cit., note 5, p. 151.

5 Variation, Privity and Law Reform

ROGER HALSON

Introduction

It seems that the doctrine of privity of contract is as simple to state as it is to disparage. For the doctrine which states that a contract cannot confer rights or impose obligations on anyone who is not a party to it has attracted much critical attention.[1] The judiciary have been untypically strident in their comments. Lord Diplock in *Swain v Law Society* referred to the restrictions upon the recognition of third party rights imposed by the doctrine of privity as an "anachronistic shortcoming that has for many years been regarded as a reproach to English private law".[2] Some senior members of the judiciary have even been moved openly to threaten its abrogation if the legislature does not take a lead.[3]

> If one had to contemplate a further long period of Parliamentary procrastination, this house might find it necessary to deal with [the matter]...If the opportunity arises, I hope the House will reconsider *Tweddle v Atkinson*[4] and the other cases which stand guard over it.

Academics have been no less pressing in their criticism.[5] Perhaps the best evidence of this is the way the doctrine is treated in standard contract texts. These generally rehearse the rule quickly by reference to *Tweedle v Atkinson*[6] and *Dunlop Pneumatic Tyre Co. v Selfridge & Co Ltd*[7] and then move on to a lengthy list of exceptions and avoidance techniques. The apparent imbalance between the area of application of the rule itself and that covered by its exceptions is not amenable to precise measurement but one is left with the intuition that in the law of contract it is probably rivalled only by the parole evidence rule as the principle which admits of the most extensive list of exceptions.[8]

83

The problems posed by a strict application of the doctrine of privity of contract have been addressed in a number of jurisdictions.[9] In the United States the Restatement (Second) Section 302 recognises the right of an "intended beneficiary" to enforce an obligation contained in a contract to which he was not a party.[10] Third parties may also acquire rights under the doctrine of promissory estoppel.[11] Other common law systems have proceeded by way of legislative reform e.g. the New Zealand Contracts (Privity) Act 1982, the Western Australia Property Law Act 1969 section 11 and the Queensland Property Law Act 1974 section 55. Civilian systems of law have long recognised third parties' rights under contracts. In Scotland a *ius quaesitium tertio* is recognised,[12] and in France Article 1121 which contained two narrow exceptions relating to contracts with penalty clauses and contracts which provide for the payment of an annuity has been developed by the courts into a more general principle for the benefit of third parties.[13] The German Civil Code recognises the concept of contracts for the benefit of third parties with supplemental provisions to protect, in certain circumstances, promisors from actions for specific performance and to avoid the situation where there can be no recovery because the person who has suffered loss has no right to sue and the person who has a right to sue has suffered no loss.[14]

Notwithstanding threats as to the future, the present response of the English courts to the perceived inadequacies of a restrictive doctrine of privity has been to chip away at its edges; that is with the notable exception of Lord Denning, who characteristically, and ultimately unsuccessfully,[15] launched a full frontal assault on the citadel of privity in *Drive Yourself Hire Co (London) Ltd v Strutt*.[16] According to current fashion various devices have been used to curb the full rigour of the doctrine. The concept of the trust has come[17] and gone[18] despite the able advocacy of Arthur Corbin.[19] The possibility of a limited exception where a promisee may recover in respect of the losses of others[20] has had an equivocal reception.[21] The flexibility of the equitable remedy of specific performance has been used to good effect when circumstances permit[22] as has the stay of action.[23] In relation to third parties obtaining the benefit of exemption clauses in contracts to which they are not parties, the traditional panacea for all known contract ills, the collateral contract,[24] has been put to new work,[25] accompanied by a warning that it comes free from the associated restrictions of offer, acceptance etc.[26] However much has been left to the parties themselves who through felicitous drafting may call in aid one of the above techniques or perhaps provide for an assignment or create a relationship of agent and principal between promisee and third party. Such solutions tend to require a high degree of legal knowledge to be available at the stage of contract negotiation which of course may be the case in commercial arrangements but is unlikely to be so in relation to contracts involving consumers. In the consumer[27] as well as the commercial context[28] the law of tort may provide assistance.

All the techniques referred to above operate to qualify the strict application of the rule of privity which prevents a third party from obtaining the benefit of a provision in a contract to which he is not a party. However the other aspect of the doctrine of privity, which provides that burdens may not be imposed on those who are not parties to a contract, always receives less attention; in the second paragraph of their Consultation Paper the Law Commission declare it to be "self evidently desirable". So indeed it may be in most of the contexts in which it is applied. Whether this is so in every context may depend upon the position taken on more fundamental questions like whether the law of contract is about the imposition of external standards of fair conduct on citizens.[29] However what we can say at present is that a carefully crafted exception to this self evident proposition may on occasion be used to good effect to remedy the commercial inconvenience caused by the benefit side of the doctrine of privity. Lord Denning's masterful dissenting judgment in *Scruttons v Midland Silicones*[30] is as eloquent a proof of this as can be found.

This discontent with the doctrine of privity has stirred law reform agencies in England more than once. In 1937 the Law Revision Committee's Sixth Interim Report recommended that where a contract expressly conferred a benefit on a third party the third party should, subject to any defence which the promisee would be entitled to raise against the promisor, be able to enforce the promise in her own name. These recommendations have influenced a number of the Commonwealth developments already mentioned e.g. those in Queensland and Western Australia.[31] It has occasioned surprise that the Law Revision Committee's proposals to reform the doctrine of privity have remained unimplemented in their country of origin, not least because they were the least controversial proposals contained in their report and other proposals were acted upon.[32]

However in 1991 the Law Commission issued a Consultation Paper[33] which again addressed the question of reform of the doctrine of privity. It is an aspect of their proposals which this essay will address, the circumstances in which the original promisor and promisee may vary a promise which was intended to benefit a third party. The next section examines the provisional recommendations of the Law Commission. However, it is interesting to note that there remains a trend in favour of reform in those jurisdictions which have not already enacted it. For example the Manitoba Law Reform Commission in its Report No 80. of 1993 Privity of Contract, has proposed a draft Privity Act which would permit third parties to enforce contractual promises made in their favour and for their benefit. The English Law Commission's Consultation Paper will have an important role to play in informing the deliberations of foreign agencies charged with similar tasks.

The Law Commission Consultation Paper

At the core of the Law Commission's Consultation Paper is the proposal that if contractors want to create legally enforceable rights in third parties the law should facilitate this. The test adopted is the so-called "double intention test"; enforceable rights are created where the contracting parties intend that a third party should receive *both* the benefit of the promised performance *and* a legal obligation enforceable by them.[34] Where this test is satisfied the rights created against the contracting promisor should include where appropriate the right to receive the promised performance, to claim remedies in respect of late or defective performance and to rely on any exempting provisions in the contract.[35] The third party's rights are to be governed by the contract and so will be affected by the validity of the contract and also be subject to any defences, set-offs and counterclaims which would have been available to the promisor in respect of any action brought against him by the promisee.[36] Futher it is proposed that third party rights may be created even though the third party is neither in existence nor ascertained at the time the contract is made.[37] Also it is recommended that all existing exceptions be retained.[38]

These definite proposals are a contrast to other key issues where the Law Commission prefers to canvass possibilities and seek further views. These include: whether modification of the original promise in favour of a third party should be permitted when the third party has accepted or adopted it or has materially relied on it, whether the contracting parties, or at least the promisee, should have actual, constructive, or no knowledge of any such acceptance, adoption or material reliance and whether these concepts should have any relevance where the contract permits modification even where there is evidence of third party acceptance, adoption or material reliance or where the third party is actually aware of such reservation.[39] However the Law Commission did recommend that there was no need for a residual power in the courts to order the variation or discharge of a contract for reasons of fairness.[40]

What is more interesting and, perhaps, more revealing than the Law Commissions's proposals and requests for further comment, is the way in which they approached their task i.e. the process of reasoning that produced the proposals and requests. Key to the Law Commission's approach is their view that reform of the doctrine of privity can be dissociated from reform of the doctrine of consideration.[41]

The Law Commission endorse the view that the two doctrines are distinct both as a matter of authority and as one of principle. As to authority it is thought that the approach of Viscount Haldane in *Dunlop v Selfridge*[42] who regards as separate the rules that "only a person who is a party to a contract can sue on it" and "a person with whom a contract not under seal has been made" is only "able to enforce it [if] consideration [has] been given by him to the promisor or to some other person at the promisor's request"[43] represents the balance of authority.[44] Consideration and privity are also thought to address separate issues of policy: the doctrine of consideration is primarily concerned with the types of promises that can be enforced while the doctrine of privity relates to who can enforce a contract.[45] As one modern writer puts it, consideration is a test of enforceability while privity determines the range of liability.[46] In particular the Law

Commission is quick to dismiss the circular reasoning which is sometimes concealed in attempts to derive the doctrine of privity from first principles of contract. Typical is that of Sir William Anson who in 1876 said that the doctrine of privity "is not only established by decided cases, but seems to flow from the very conception which we form of contract."[47] However Patrick Atiyah has exposed a very real danger that such attempts to derive the doctrine of privity often do little more than elaborate the consequences of their own unsubstantiated assumptions: it is assumed that only someone who supplies consideration can be a party and then deduced that someone cannot be treated as a party because he has not supplied any consideration.[48]

This then gives the Law Commission the starting point for their discussion of principle. They investigate a number of related and overlapping factors which may possibly be said to justify the doctrine of privity. These include: parties may circumvent the effects of the rule by careful drafting, contracts are personal transactions, promisors should not be liable to two actions, so called "mutuality" of rights between the contracting parties and the third party,[49] parity between third party beneficiaries and other gratuitous donees,[50] if third parties could enforce contracts made for their benefit, the rights of contracting parties to cancel or modify such rights would be affected and that privity provides a valuable control mechanism on the potential liability of a contracting party. The Law Commission conclude[51] that these factors do not offer a sufficient reason for retaining the rule that third parties may not receive an enforceable benefit under a contract to which they are not a party.

The merits of these various arguments have been examined elsewhere.[52] All except the penultimate factor are broader than the subject of this essay. On this point the Law Commission recognise that the reforms proposed might prejudice the rights of the original contracting parties to modify their contract without the consent of the third party. However no reason is given to justify this limitation upon the freedom of contracting parties to consensually vary their contract. Of course it may be possible to create third party rights which do not take precedence over the contracting party's power to modify.[53] The reform proposed can be framed in a number of ways which respect, to differing degrees, the rights of the original contractors to vary their agreement. Indeed the full spectrum of possible positions is reflected in the reforms adopted by the various jurisdictions examined.[54] France and Scotland seem to occupy the two polar positions on the spectrum: in France third party rights are subject to the unilateral revocation of the promisee while the Scottish Law Commission concluded that a term in favour of a third party should be irrevocable in the absence of an express reservation by the original contractors of their right to vary. Other jurisdictions adopt intermediary positions: in Western Australia, following the recommendations of the English Law Revision Committee, the contracting parties are free to modify their agreement until the third party adopts the contract, in Queensland they are free to modify their agreement until the third party accepts or assents to the contract and in New Zealand they are seen to modify their agreement until the third party materially alters his position in reliance on the contract. Further hybrid solutions may be adopted: under the American Restatement (Second) third party rights become irrevocable when the third party either materially changes his position in justifiable reliance or brings suit or manifests assent at the request of the promisor or promisee.

The Place of Theory

In 1915 Samuel Williston said:[55]

> In no department of the law has a more obstinate and persistent battle between practice and theory been waged than in regard to the question: whether a right of action accrues to a third party from a contract made by others for his benefit.

Whether Williston's view of what constitutes theory is as broad as that which now pertains is perhaps debatable. However it is apparent that the Law Commission would take issue with the present implications of his statement. They state:[56]

> ... the development of English contract law has been pragmatic and not the outcome of one particular theory ...

The Law Commission then proceed to examine[57] very briefly the implications for the doctrine of privity of a "will" theory of contract, a "bargain" theory and a reliance based model and conclude that a rule excluding third parties from enforcing benefits conferred on them by contracts to which they are not a party is not a logical corollary of subscription to any particular model or theory of contract. In their own words:[58]

> the third party rule is not a necessary part of any of the supposed theoretical foundations of contractual liability.

This view is correct. However what is disappointing is that while the Law Commission's failure to take a position on the relative merits of different theories of contract does not prevent the recognition of an exception to the third party rule it does make it difficult, and in some ways impossible, to give clear expression to the limits of that exception. This is especially true in respect of the variation of the original contract without the consent of the third party beneficiary. So while theory can be ignored as regards the abstract acceptance of enforceable third party rights, the practical value of such acceptance is highly questionable when the limits of the new principle cannot be defined. The importance of theory in relation to identifying the exact time when a third party may be said to have acquired an enforceable right is at least conceded in a footnote.[59] There is no full discussion in the report of the importance of theory to the problems raised by variation on the part of the original contractors; it is to be regretted that theory raises its head so briefly and is dismissed so curtly as relevant only to second order questions. It could be hoped that at the very point when the Law Commissions proposals end and further views are sought the need for deeper reflection would be recognised.[60]

What reasons can there be for the failure to address such important questions. One explanation and one justification come to mind. The explanation is that the failure to take a position on questions of why we enforce promises follows from the initial doctrinal separation of consideration and privity. As soon as the argument is accepted that privity can be reformed independently of the doctrine of consideration attention is diverted away from any questions as to why promises should be enforced, with the consequences we have already described.

The justification is related to the explanation. It is that bodies engaged in law reform will always be tempted to avoid controversy in order to ease the passage of any proposed reform. The hazardous nature of legislative reform is amply reflected in the history of a number of recent measures. For instance a Carriage of Goods by Sea Bill was lost in 1992 when Parliament was dissolved. The potential hazards here are greatest when a measure is introduced by a private member.[61] However this surely will not do. A draft bill to reform the doctrine of privity must be finalised at some time . This bill will have to define the rights of the original contractors to vary their contract and this simply cannot be done until some basic questions are asked.

Contract as Promise and the Reliance Model

It would be misleading to claim that a discussion of the will theory of contract as propounded by Charles Fried and the reliance and benefit based approach associated with Patrick Atiyah could seek to represent the wide range of theoretical discussions of the law of contract which have been produced in recent years.[62] Fortunately such an overview is not necessary for present purposes. For it is not claimed that the brief discussion which follows of these two approaches is the larger exercise which the Law Commission should have undertaken. Rather these two approaches will be discussed to *illustrate* how a consideration of theory might be able to provide answers to unresolved questions. To arrive at a singular answer a choice must be made between the merits of competing theories. It is not possible here to evaluate those merits or make that choice.

The will theory of obligation holds that the law should give effect to the will of the individual to be bound.[63] Thus the law should enforce any promise which expresses the free will of a party even in the absence of any element of benefit or reliance. Charles Fried's Contract as Promise is sub-titled "A Theory of Contractual Obligation" and, in the tradition of the will theory, argues that contractual obligations are self imposed. Promising involves the deliberate invocation of trust in the future actions of the promisor, it involves the invocation of a convention which gives moral grounds to justify another in expecting that which is promised.[64] In Fried's own words:[65]

> By promising we transform a choice that was morally neutral into one that is morally compelled. Morality, which must be permanent and beyond our particular will if the grounds for our willing are to be secure, is itself invoked, moulded to allow us better to work that particular will.

According to Fried promising is a voluntary activity both on the part of promisor and promisee; a promise must be accepted though, of course, acceptance may be inferred.[66] When this requirement of acceptance is conjoined with the moral force of promising it justifies an exception to the doctrine of privity when a contractor promises to confer a benefit on a third party and that third party accepts the promise.[67] For Fried this is;[68]

> ...acceptance in its purest form, untinctured by any element of counterpromise or exchange. It is the very operative act of acquiescing in the promissory benefit that ... is necessary to complete a binding promise.

It seems that for Fried from the moment of acceptance by the third party the obligation owed to her may not be varied by the contracting parties without her consent. According to the Restatement (Second) of Contracts Section 311 the original contractors cannot vary the obligation assumed towards the third party once she has manifested assent to it; however the same is true where she materially changes her position in reliance on it or brings suit on it. The French Civil Code and the Queensland Property Law Act 1974 adopt positions which prevent variation after acceptance or assent alone and so conform more closely to Fried's analysis.[69]

Patrick Atiyah's name is associated with a theory of contract[70] that is very different in emphasis to that of Charles Fried.[71] Atiyah thinks that most modern contract scholars would agree that:[72]

> the law must accommodate countervailing values deriving from the pursuit of collective goals and from the paternalistic belief that collective judgments about the best interests of individuals are sometimes more likely to be correct than the individual's own judgment.

This view draws parallels between the law of contract on the one hand and that of tort and restitution on the other. Tort, which aims to compensate individuals for wrongful harm and restitution which seeks to reverse unjust enrichment both involve the external imposition of standards of behaviour. So too according to Atiyah does the law of contract.

Such a view has clear implications for the variation of their contract by the original contractors in a way which affects third party rights. For just as Patrick Atiyah would question the enforcement of an unrelied upon wholly executory contract, so presumably, in a three party situation, he would question the enforcement of any obligation in favour of third parties until there was an act of reasonable reliance. The further corollary of this is presumably that thereafter the original contract may only be varied with the consent of the third party. This is the position adopted in New Zealand under Section 5 of the Contracts (Privity) Act 1982.

Conclusion

The Law Commission have made a very strong case for legislative reform of the rule that third parties to contracts cannot generally enforce benefits conferred on them by that contract. However a more difficult task lies ahead; to draft proposals which marry the desire to give third parties enforceable rights with a proper respect for the right of the original contractors to vary their contract as they wish. The tension between these aims will only be resolved by addressing some very basic questions about why we enforce contracts, which may in turn suggest to them that some "self evidently desirable" principles are not so. But that, of course, is another story.

Notes

1. For richer schemes of classification see e.g. Adams and Brownsword (1990) 10 L.S. 12 at p. 13.
2. [1983] 1 A.C. 598 at p. 611.
3. *Woodar Investment Development Ltd v Wimpey Construction UK Ltd* [1980] 1 All E.R. 571 at p. 591. The first sentence is itself a quotation from Lord Reid's speech in *Beswick v. Beswick* [1968] A.C. 58 at p. 72.
4. (1861) 1 B & S 393.
5. See e.g. Corbin (1930) 46 L.Q.R. 12, Furmston (1960) M.L.R. 373, Markessinis (1987) 103 L.Q.R. 354, Adams and Brownsword (1990) 10 L.S. 12 and Beyleveld and Brownsword (1991) 54 M.L.R. 48.
6. (1861) 1 B & S 393.
7. [1915] A.C. 847.
8. See Treitel, The Law of Contract (9th ed. 1995) where the rule is stated in two paragraphs and the exception listed by letter run from a to m. Indeed it has been suggested that the exception that parol evidence is admissible when the written agreement does not record the whole of the parties' bargain is itself so wide as to consume the rule itself. See Law Commission Report on the Parol Evidence Rule (Law Comm. No. 154).

9.   See generally the appendix to the Law Commission Consultation Paper No. 121 (1991), Privity of Contract: Contracts for the Benefit of Third Parties and see the valuable discussions in *Trident General v McNeice Bros* [1988] 80 A.L.J.R. 574.

10.   *Lawrence v Fox* 20 N.Y. 268 (1859).

11.   *Hoffman v Red Owl Stores Inc* 133 NW 2d 267 (1965).

12.   Though its requirements are subject to some doubt. In their Consultation Paper No 121, Privity of Contract: Contracts for the Benefit of Third Parties, the Law Commission suggest that this may be the reason why in *Junior Books v Veitchi* [1983] 1 A.C. 520 the owner did not seek to argue that he was a third party beneficiary of the contract between the contractor and the sub-contractor. However this is more likely to be explained by the fact that the owners had compromised a series of claims arising from breaches of the contract between the main contractor and the sub-contractor. If this compromise amounted to an assumption of risk by the owner in respect of any loss that might result from the floor proving defective, the result in the case would appear to be unjustified. See Atiyah, An Introduction to the Law of Contract (5th ed.) 1995 p. 383 n. 40. Contra Beyleveld and Brownsword loc. cit. p. 50.

13.   See Nicholas, French Law of Contract, (1982) at p. 180.

14.   The principle of "transferred loss" discussed by Robert Goff L.J. in the Court of Appeal in *the Aliakmon* [1986] A.C. 785 at [1985] Q.B. 350.

15.   The rule was reaffirmed by the House of Lords in *Midland Silicones v Scruttons Ltd* [1962] A.C. 446, Lord Denning dissenting.

16.   [1954] 1 Q.B. 250.

17.   *Les Affreteurs Réunis S.A. v Leopold Walford* (London) Ltd [1919] A.C. 801.

18.   *Vanderpitte v Preferred Accident Insurance Co* [1933] A.C. 70 and *Re Schebsman* [1944] ch. 83.

19.   (1930) 46 L.Q.R. 12.

20.   *Jackson v Horizon Holidays* [1975] 1 W.L.R. 1468.

21.   *Woodar Investment Development Ltd v Wimpey Construction (U.K.)* [1980] 1 W.L.R. 277. Lord Wilberforce at p. 283 did not disagree with the result but was unsure as to how that result was arrived at.

22.   *Beswick v Beswick* [1968] A.C. 58.

23.   *Gore v Van der Lann* [1967] 2 Q.B. 31 although the provision the third party sought to take the benefit of in that case was rendered void by statute. However see also *Snelling v John G. Snelling* [1973] Q.B. 87.

24.   Wedderburn [1959] C.L.J. 58.

25.   *New Zealand Shipping Company v A.M. Satterthwaite & Co Ltd (The Eurymedon)* [1975] A.C. 154.

26.   *The New York Star* [1981] 1 W.L.R. 138.

27.   *Ross v Caunters* [1980] ch. 297.

28.   *Junior Books v Veitchi* [1983] 1 A.C. 520.

29. Infra.
30. [1962] A.C. 446.
31. Supra.
32. See Beatson (1995) C.L.P. 1.
33. Law Comm., No. 196.
34. Para 6.3.
35. Ibid. para 6.6.
36. Ibid. para 6.10.
37. Ibid. para 6.8.
38. Ibid. para. 6.18.
39. Ibid para. 6.12.
40. Ibid. para 6.12.
41. Ibid. para 2.10.
42. [1915] A.C. 847.
43. Ibid. p. 853.
44. Op. cit. para 2.6.
45. Ibid. para 2.9.
46. See Collins, The Law of Contract (2nd ed.) 1993 chs 3 & 12 and especially p. 288.
47. Principles of the Law of Contract (1879) at p. 195 quoted by Deane J. in *Trident General Insurance Co Ltd v. McNeice Bros Pty Ltd* (1988) 62 A.L.J.R. 508 at p. 523.
48. Consideration in Contracts: A Fundamental Restatement (1971) Contra. Furmston (1960) 23 M.L.R. 373 at p.384.
49. "It would be a monstrous proposition to say that a person was a party to the contract for the purpose of suing upon it for his own advantage, and not a party to it for the purpose of being sued" per Compton J. in *Tweddle v. Atkinson* (1861) 1 B & S 393.
50. Which may be an aspect of mutuality see Adams and Brownsword (1990) 10 L.S. 12 at pp. 23-4 and Collins, op cit. pp. 288-9.
51. Op. cit. para 4.4.
52. For general discussions of supposed justifications of privity doctrines see Pearson (1983) 5 Otago L. Rev. 316, Adams and Brownsword loc. cit., Collins op. cit. ch. 12.
53. Collins op. cit. pp. 287-8.
54. Loc. cit. Appendix.
55. 15 Harv. L. Rev. 767.
56. Op. cit. para. 4.5.
57. Loc. cit. para 4.5.
58. Loc. cit. para 4.5.
59. Loc. cit. p. 72 n. 17.

Of course the choice of theory will affect the circumstances in which C would be accorded a legal right to enforce performance. On a reliance theory, he would not have any right until he acted in reliance, whereas under an expectation theory no such reliance would be necessary.

60. See supra. text preceding n. 38.
61. E.g. Peter Thurnham's Private Member's Bill to reform privity of contract in commercial leases.
62. For such an overview see the materials collected in S.Wheeler & J.Shaw Contract Law, Cases Materials and Commentary 1994 and Collins,op. cit. especially ch. 3.
63. See Pound (1959) 33 Tulane Law Rev. 455.
64. See Fried op. cit. ch. 2.
65. Op. cit. p. 8.
66. Op. cit. ch. 4.
67. Op. cit. p. 44.
68. Op. cit. p. 45.
69. See Law Commission Consultation Paper p. 115 and appendix.
70. Atiyah: The Rise and Fall of the Freedom of Contract 1979, Essays on Contract 1986 especially ch. 2, An Introduction to the Law of Contract (5th ed.) 1995 especially ch. 1.
71. For comments by each on the other's work see Fried op. cit. ch. 1 and Atiyah, Essays on Contract 1988 ch. 6.
72. Atiyah, Essays on Contract 1986 ch. 6 at p. 146.

6 Great Art Living Dangerously? Legal and Empirical Issues in the Lending of Works of Art

NORMAN PALMER

Introduction

The aim of this paper is to describe some of the legal and practical issues which arise from the lending and borrowing of works of art, and to illustrate the distance between those sets of issues. The subject is remarkable for several reasons. Most art loans are high-value transactions involving objects of exceptional cultural and emotional importance. They play a crucial role in widening public access to art while posing risks, both physical and political, to an irreplaceable subject matter. In some areas, those hazards have been thought sufficiently acute to attract governmental intervention.[1] For these and other reasons, the conduct of art loans is a matter of public interest and not merely a commercial affair.

For all their distinctive features, art loans have largely escaped critical legal analysis. With the exception of those practitioners who are instructed in specific cases, or those who work as in-house counsel to museums or galleries,[2] most lawyers have disregarded them. Outside the United States, where legal analysis of cultural property issues is generally more advanced, there is an almost complete dearth of legal writing.

There are several possible reasons. One is the general legal unimportance of chattel lending. True chattel loans are gratuitous bailments,[3] and gratuitous relations are (for the most part) commercially marginal.[4] Another is the lack of judicial analysis. The last significant judgment on the rights of lender and borrower was delivered in New Zealand in 1974.[5] The case involved the lending of a car to an inebriated woman and her ability to plead contributory negligence and volenti non fit injuria in defence to the lender's claim; issues unlikely to be mirrored in a museum loan.[6] Although misadventures involving borrowed works of art occur, serious disputes are rare and (as between institutions, at least) never litigated.

A third reason, which may partially explain the second, is a reluctance by museum officials to consult lawyers or legal principles. So far as one can judge, this stems mainly from a failure to perceive the necessity. Many art loan agreements are made routinely without specific legal advice.[7] Each museum has standard forms for incoming and outgoing loans and normally views these as covering all realistic contingencies.[8] The official most closely involved in the management of the loan is usually the museum registrar, typically an experienced administrator with high organisational skills but no formal legal training. Such officers have little time for juridical analysis and are sometimes squeamish about lawyers, seeing them as obstructive and predatory. Lawyers, one is told, are too fond of telling museums what they cannot do and of seeing the need for remunerative work.[9] The following reactions are gleaned from a survey conducted between 1993 and 1995:

> [Lawyers] tend to make the process more complicated, negotiations become more complex, every point seems a problem generating much more work. In short, they make the process slow and inflexible.

> [W]e are somewhat suspicious of lawyers, who appear unsympathetic to our needs. We do not want something produced which is too legalistic and cannot be understood by non-lawyers.

> They have a role to play but the tail must not wag the dog.

Allied to these reservations is a deep belief in the clanship of museums and in their ability to resolve loan disputes among themselves by a judicious appeal to professional loyalty and common interest. No observer, schooled in the adversarial rites of the common law, can fail to be impressed by the village atmosphere in which art loans are conducted, by the sense of common purpose, and by the prevalence of trust and goodwill. In the words of one official:

> [A] great number of loans take place between Art Galleries and Museums world wide ... [T]hese institutions are, however diverse their geographical situations, all very like each other. The staff in them have common professional goals, and speak a common professional language. Over and above the rules laid down on pieces of paper - loan forms etc - all these people understand very well how the system works, what is expected of a loan or exhibition and what it is all about.

The same official was quick to stress the virtues of pragmatism in a museum's relations with its private lenders. On matters of authenticity, for example, where lender and borrower differ about the authorship of a work,[10] the prospect of litigation was considered so remote as to be negligible:

> Of course curators may quite frequently disagree with owners ... about the attribution of works. Extreme tact may be required to avoid giving offence, but this is a social not a legal problem ... The owner's opinion as to who did or did not paint the picture would be completely irrelevant. Private owners have enough to put up with already from Museums bombarding them with requests to borrow. If owners were also to be held legally liable for attributions, and were punished for any mistakes - or dissident opinions - no one would ever lend at all.[11]

In negotiating loans, most museum officials pay the closest regard to non-legal or quasi-legal considerations: valuation, insurance, security measures, humidity control, orderly paperwork, practical redress in the event of misconduct and the maintenance of good personal relations. The last two are particularly emphasised. A museum official may react with bemusement on being asked, for example, why loan forms make no express provision for the legal consequences of a borrower's misuse of the loaned object or breach of security conditions. To the offical, the answer is simple, and wholly divorced from such legal phenomena as deviation from the bailment, insurer's liability, repudiatory breach, revival of the immediate right to possession, conditions and innominate terms. If necessary, the lender withdraws the object and/or refuses to lend to the borrower in future. The mere prospect of these sanctions is normally enough.

Such attitudes can deter museums not only from litigating but from seeking precautionary legal advice. A reluctance to litigate is, of course, sound policy; a refusal to contemplate it may not be. Here, as elsewhere, it is hard to banish the suspicion that a lack of curiosity about theoretical issues has practical risks. One overseas official, who professed concern about an unforeseen potential ground of liability and was asked how she would now approach the problem, replied that she would wait until a case arose. Other officials, asked to describe their practice when terms in the loan forms of lender and borrower are at odds, said that the solution is simple: each side signs and returns the other's form, and in that way the paper-work is kept in order. Several officials stated a preference for leaving the governing law of the loan unspecified, on the ground that specific consideration of this issue is likely to retard negotiations. It is even hinted that, to preserve harmony, each party might be permitted to stipulate its own domicile as choice of governing law. By such avenues do pigeons come home to roost.

This gap between theory and practice may be regretted for other reasons. To common lawyers at least, the gratuitous bailment is an interesting hybrid. The art loan may be its most costly and sophisticated manifestation. It would clearly be beneficial if the assumptions and concerns of those conducting such loans were better understood. Moreover, art loans carry great benefits, both temporal and cultural. They are a useful diplomatic tool, and can help to marginalise title disputes.[12] Some loans generate substantial revenue in the form of loan payments by the borrowing museum, or in entrance money and reproduction fees.[13] The lender may be attracted by free storage and insurance, and general relief from the burdens of ownership.[14] For a private lender, a carefully orchestrated loan can enhance the provenance and sale profile of a work; some American museums provide for a commission payment on works sold while on loan to them.[15] More cynically, a public loan may make a work of dubious proprietary origin sufficiently discoverable to activate any relevant limitation period. All these factors fortify the case for a strong, accessible and internationally acceptable law on art loans.

Reference has already been made to the case against greater legal intervention. It finds colloquial expression in the aphorism "If it ain't broke, don't fix it". There may, perhaps, be difficulty in applying this adage to latent defects, into which class some deficiencies of our system of art loans may fall. Museum officials, as we have seen, stress the internal strengths of the existing regime: the capacity for amicable resolution of differences, the compendious nature of loan forms, the wealth of communal experience in administering loans and a vast record of uneventful transactions. Arguably, however, none of these factors fully warrants a disregard of abstract legal principle. The terms of the loan form may not cover every event and may not apply to those events which are expressly addressed if procedural error leads to non-incorporation. Nor can one be sure that modern museum managers will necessarily favour the amicable or non-confrontational solution of differences. For these and other reasons, institutions would be wise to distance themselves from the forward planning policy once ascribed to Lars Porsena of Clusium.[16]

The legal character of art loans

The legal concept of commodatum, or loan, is familiar to both common and civil law. In England, it first found authoritative expression in Holt C.J.'s exposition of the principles of bailment in *Coggs v Bernard*.[17] The Chief Justice had this to say about commodatum:

> As to the second sort of bailment, viz. commodatum or lending gratis, the borrower is bound to the strictest care and diligence to keep the goods, so as to restore them back again to the lender, because the bailee has a benefit by the use of them, so as if the bailee be guilty of the least neglect, he will be answerable; as if a man should lend another a horse, to go westward, or for a month; if the bailee go northward, or keep the horse above expiration of the month, the bailee will be chargeable; because he has made use of the horse contrary to the trust he was lent to him under, and it may be if the horse had been used no otherwise than he was lent, that accident would not have befallen him... But if the bailee put this

horse in his stable, and he was stolen from thence, the bailee shall not be answerable for him. But if he or his servant leave the house or stable doors open, and the thieves take the opportunity of that, and steal the horse, he will be chargeable; because the neglect gave the thieves the occasion to steal the horse. Bracton says, the bailee must use the utmost care, but yet he shall not be chargeable, where there is such a force as he cannot resist.

Inherent in Holt C.J.'s analysis were four apparent assumptions. The first was that a chattel loan was a contract.[18] The second was that, for a bailment to constitute a loan, the borrower must be the sole party to benefit. The third was that the duty of care owed by the borrower[19] was more exacting than that imposed by a mutually beneficial bailment.[20] The fourth (less clearly stated) was that a borrower who deviated from the essential terms of the loan incurred a strict liability to the lender.

Three further qualities were added by later authority. One was that a lender owed no liability for injury, damage or loss caused by a defect in the chattel unless he or she knew of that defect at the time of the loan.[21] Another (favoured by the general law of bailment,[22] but never specifically applied to loans) was that the borrower was estopped from denying the lender's title.[23] A third (also part of the general law)[24] was that the borrower could sue any third party who committed a wrong against the chattel during the loan, and could recover from that third party full damages as if the borrower were the owner. Such damages were then held for the lender, after deduction of the borrower's personal loss. Even so, as against a wrongdoer the borrower's possession counted as title.[25]

The first and second assumptions (contract and gratuitousness) were incompatible once the common law evolved the doctrine of consideration. In New Zealand, the contractual analysis of gratuitous loans has been roundly rejected for want of consideration.[26] Chattel loans are said in consequence to have nothing to do with the law of contract.[27] Other ambiguities have, almost certainly, vanished over the past century. It appears from general authority that the duties of the parties to a gratuitous bailment now lie in negligence rather than in some greater or lesser degree of care.[28] If art loans are true loans they are non-contractual, having no common law content beyond reciprocal duties of care. They are creatures of tort and bailment, but not of contract.

But the question arises: is the typical art loan a true gratuitous bailment by way of commodatum? It is submitted that, for reasons already noted,[29] this is improbable. Loan is a bailment which exclusively benefits the borrower: the bailor lends as a favour, getting nothing in return. Many lenders of art, even if they make no direct charge, expect to benefit from the loan. The result is that an art loan may generate consideration, and therefore constitute a contract as well as a bailment.

A contractual analysis would accord with the sophisticated nature of many loan agreements, painstakingly forged by powerful parties promoting valuable interests. Even under routine loans, obligations are likely to be spelt out by the standard loan agreement, and resort to the common law of bailment is unlikely. In the words of a curator, bailment is nearly always displaced by contract. Other than in the case of "old loans",[30] curators rarely have recourse to the simple law of bailment.

Two further questions then arise. What sort of bailment is the standard art loan, if not a true gratuitous loan, and what difference does it make?

The theoretical difference, at least, is substantial. If art loans are contracts, supplementary promises made by the lender (for example, as to the condition of the object or its authenticity) are contractually binding. Their enforceability no longer turns on the exotic ambiguity of gratuitous bailment and its cloudy relationship with tort.[31] If compelled to reclassify the relationship according to Holt C.J.'s categories, we would probably identify it as a bailment by way of hire ("*locatio et conductio rei*").[32] Under such a bailment, the bailee is allowed the use and enjoyment of a chattel in return for a benefit to the bailor.

Interesting consequences may follow. First, the borrower may be entitled to a secure term of possession, rather than being at the mercy of the lender's change of heart.[33] Secondly, the lender may be deemed to warrant title, so that a borrower who is ousted by a valid third party claim can claim damages from the lender.[34] Thirdly, the lender may be answerable for breach of statutory implied conditions as to the object's compliance with its description, its fitness for its intended purpose and its merchantable quality; implied promises which (strange as it may seem) may make a lender strictly liable in damages if the borrowed work proves inauthentic or otherwise unfit for exhibition.[35] As a bailee for reward the borrower must also take reasonable care of the object[36] and must prove, in the event of loss or damage, that these events are not due to any breach of that duty; if such evidence is not forthcoming, the borrower is presumed to be at fault.[37] For these and similar reasons,[38] it is unfortunate that the legal designation of the agreement does not receive closer attention, either within loan agreements themselves or in general literature on art loans.

Universality of the loan concept

It will be recalled that Holt C.J.'s exposition of the law of commodatum purported to derive[39] from Roman law.[40] A similar concept exists in other European countries. For example, private loans under Spanish law are governed by the rules of "*comodato*" contained in Articles 1741-1742 of the Civil Code.[41] Private loans in France attract Articles 1875-1981 of the Code Civile which deal with the "*prêt à usage ou commodat*". A similar concept is recognised under Article 305 CA of the Swiss Civil Code, Sections 598 to 606 of the German Civil Code and Title XVIII, Articles 710 to 719 of the Polish Civil Code. The legal characteristics of these transactions are broadly similar to those of the English commodatum, although European systems tend to be more specific (and restrictive) as to the circumstances in which the object may be withdrawn.

This rare coincidence of common and civil law, in an area crucial to cultural exchange, might be thought conducive to harmonisation. And yet there is little sign that these common juristic roots have led to any meaningful international co-operation. One looks in vain for any over-arching legal instrument or statement of principle. Individual treaties, regulating specific loans, are not uncommon;[42] multilateral agreements are virtually unknown.[43] This is regrettable, because there are many dimensions of the loan agreement which might profit from such treatment. This is particularly so, given the reluctance in some quarters to articulate vital aspects of the agreement.[44]

Matters of common provision

Security and the duty of care

Foremost among the matters for which lenders and borrowers conventionally provide are safety and security. It is common for loan agreements to prescribe elaborate procedures and precautions, which may be directed both to ensuring the integrity of the object during the loan and determining its condition at critical points.[45] These requirements are highly transaction-specific and are almost as diverse as the objects themselves; little would be gained by detailed exposition. What is interesting is the general failure to spell out the legal consequences of breach. At common law, one might expect a serious departure from the agreed mode of treatment of a bailed object to constitute a deviation,[46] forfeiting the borrower's right of possession, rendering the borrower strictly liable for all ensuing losses regardless of negligence, and possibly invalidating the borrower's normal exclusion clauses. Loan agreements rarely specify such consequences, probably for four reasons. First, there is a greater reliance on non-legal sanctions than in ordinary commercial contracts: to break the agreement is to jeopardise future loans. Secondly, most institutional loan agreements are underpinned by insurance, or by some form of public indemnity, which will often exclude subrogation; the lender has correspondingly less reason than most to stipulate remedies in the agreement. Thirdly, the possibility of a deliberate and self-seeking breach ranks low in the parties' calculations; other departures from the loan terms can normally be redressed by professional means. Fourthly, the question of legal remedy may simply not have occurred to the parties. In this consideration lies, perhaps, a lesson for lawyers as much as for curators. So far as one can judge, loan terms are drafted in the expectation that they will be observed, not broken. The agreement is approached as a non-confrontational code of guidance rather than as a catalogue of imperatives and sanctions. That does not mean that the stipulations in the agreement are taken any less seriously. It simply means that the law plays no part in the parties' calculations as to the machinery for ensuring observance.

Duties of care, indemnities and insurance are another field of express provision. It is relatively uncommon for an English loan agreement to spell out the abstract standard of care demanded of the borrower, although such definitions are not unknown. The practice is much commoner in the United States, where a typical provision requires the borrowing museum to exercise the same degree of care of the borrowed object as it takes of its own property of similar nature.[47] Interestingly, it was held in England as early as 1834 that an unrewarded bailee[48] does not necessarily satisfy the normal duty of care by showing the same degree of care as was shown towards the bailee's own property.[49] If that degree of care were deficient, the mere fact that the bailee's property was similarly put at risk made no difference. In England, it could be argued that a clause casting the borrower's duty in terms of a subjective obligation to behave only *quam suis rebus*[50] is an attempt to exclude or restrict the normal duty of reasonable care which would arise under the bailment, so attracting the Unfair Contract Terms Act 1977[51] and requiring the borrower to show that the clause is reasonable.[52]

If the agreement is silent on the point, a borrower must exercise that degree of care which is reasonable in all the circumstances, having regard to the value, portability and disposability of the goods, any express assurance or undertaking given, the purposes of the loan and the conditions in which it is to be discharged. That is the appropriate standard where, through some reciprocal benefit, the bailment is one for reward.[53] Pure loans, which give the bailor no benefit, are without modern authority but the borrower's duty is likely to be comparable, requiring reasonable care in all the circumstances.[54] In each case, moreover, the borrower carries the burden of showing that the necessary care was taken. Curiously, even those loan agreements which spell out the duty of care make no attempt to locate the burden of proof.

Insurance

A more pivotal consideration than any abstract definition of the duty of care is that of insurance. Lenders of objects normally expect them to be insured and borrowers customarily (though not invariably) accept responsibility for this. A borrowing institution is likely to give the lender two options: to participate in the borrower's own insurance or to maintain the lender's own (extended where necessary to cover the change of location).[55] In either event, insurance will be "nail to nail", but subject to standard exclusions.[56] Where the lender elects to continue its own insurance, the borrower will normally insert in the loan agreement provisions calculated to protect it against liability to the lender's insurer. The borrower may do so in three main ways: by requiring to be added as a co-insured, by requiring that the insurer waive its subrogation rights, or by a simple exclusion of its liability to the lender. Some United States museums employ an amalgam of two (or even all three) of these devices.

Loan agreements which require the object to be insured often acknowledge that a governmental indemnity is an acceptable alternative. Such indemnities are seen as an important facilitating factor in the cross-border movement of art. Again, the subject is too complex for present analysis, but it is notable that while more countries appear to be developing indemnity schemes, there is no centralised movement towards uniformity. Formal schemes exist in the United States, the United Kingdom, Australia, New Zealand, France, The Netherlands[57] and some Scandinavian countries. In Australia, the Commonwealth (Federal) indemnity scheme is supplemented by State schemes in Victoria, Queensland and New South Wales. Outside these countries, formal indemnity arrangements are rare, but ad hoc governmental provision is occasionally made for particular loans.

The United Kingdom scheme,[58] expressed as a contract between the relevant Department of State and the lender,[59] gives the Secretary of State a right of subrogation against any person "in respect of the loss or damage" indemnified against. The indemnity requires, as conditions precedent, the incorporation of certain terms into the loan agreement; these regulate the liability of the borrower and impose a prohibition on restoration work. The indemnity does not cover certain excepted perils, viz, loss or damage arising from the following causes: war, hostilities or war-like operations; the negligence or wrongful act of the owner, his servants or agents; the condition of the object at the time of its loan to the borrower; a claim by a third party claiming to be entitled to the object; and restoration or conservation work undertaken to the object by the borrower, his servants or agents with the agreement of the owner. The exclusion of loss caused to the lender by third-party title claims has especial significance given the absence of anti-seizure legislation in the United Kingdom.[60]

General subjects of express provision

Beyond these matters, express terms of general international application are relatively uncommon. Agreements normally provide for the distribution of reproduction and other intellectual property rights,[61] and for such housekeping matters as the cost and means of transportation.[62] Another familiar provision is a prohibition on the borrower's carrying out any repair or restoration of the object.[63] The larger United States museums also make special provision for the disposal of "old loans"[64] and for the proper destination of the object on termination of the loan; typically, by conferring on the museum an unfettered discretion to dispose of uncollected and untraceable objects after a certain period, and by providing that delivery to the original deliveror shall be deemed a sufficient discharge of the museum's obligation unless the deliveror gives written authority for an alternative mode of restitution.[65] English museums tend to be silent on these points. Occasionally, standard loan agreements will require that the object be exhibited only in accordance with its character and dignity,[66] or will emphasise the discretionary nature of the museum's decision as to fact and mode of exhibition;[67] such terms are not necessarily incompatible.

Matters not commonly provided for

More interesting, perhaps, are those matters of potential dispute which are characteristically omitted from the express record of commitment. For reasons of space, only four such questions will be considered, but others could be envisaged without much difficulty.

Title

A strong example is title. In theory, much trouble can be caused to a borrower whose lender lacks title to the chattel or authority to lend it. If the country where the borrower is situated has no anti-seizure statute,[68] a third party claimant may descend on the borrower and recover the object by proving a title superior to that of the lender. Aside from litigation and management costs, the borrower may be forced to cancel an exhibition, relocate other works, destroy catalogues and reproductions and even refund sponsorship money. Such measures may offend both the borrowing institution's visiting clientele and other lenders to the same exhibition.

In theory, a borrowing museum can ensure that it recovers these losses from the lender by extracting a warranty of title.[69] And yet it is unusual to find an express term guaranteeing that the lender is the owner. The J. Paul Getty Museum in Malibu, California, includes such a term in its standard in-loan conditions, as does the Tel Aviv Museum of Art. Elsewhere, the matter is largely left unstated. This requires an ousted borrower to take refuge in the implied terms of the loan agreement.

Such resort immediately encounters two main difficulties: first, that of convincing a court that the detailed written document was not designed to be an exhaustive statement of the parties' obligations,[70] and secondly that of identifying the juridical nature of the transaction, on which the lender's obligations as to title and quiet possession may depend.

If the agreement is a bailment by way of hire, English law implies in the borrower's favour two terms of strict obligation: a condition that the lender has the right to hire the object and a warranty that the borrower will enjoy quiet possession of it during the period of hire.[71] Either term would enable a dispossessed borrower to recover damages for foreseeable loss caused by the existence of a superior title in a third party. If, on the other hand, the bailment is a true commodatum or loan, the position is less clear. Far from being entitled to sue for a want of title in the lender, the borrower may find itself estopped from denying the lender's title.[72] Arguably, the borrower may dodge the estoppel by alleging that the lender's want of title constitutes a "defect" in the chattel. In that event, it must be decided whether the lender's duty is to take reasonable care to

104

discover and warn of the (title) defect,[73] or merely to disclose those latent (title) defects of which he is aware.[74] It is improbable, in any event, that courts will impose a strict liability under a simple loan. These puzzles reflect scant credit on the law.

Few museums appear willing to contemplate legal action against a fellow institution for want of title.[75] Such risks are seen as an institutional hazard. Among national museums this pragmatism may make sense, though accountability for public money is an issue. Commercial or private borrowers may be less tolerant. Suppose that an owner lends a picture to a museum, is allowed in return to borrow something from its collection, and is then forced to disgorge the borrowed object to a third party from whom it was stolen years ago.[76] Not every borrower would react in a spirit of genial stoicism. Museums would be well advised to provide expressly for title claims.

There is a further dimension, which concerns the borrower's rights against the lender. It is uncertain whether a lender of goods is bound by a promise to grant the borrower secure possession over a stated period.[77] As with third party claims, the losses which a breach of this promise may cause the borrower are easily imagined.[78] In cases of a simple loan, the lender may be entitled to revoke the promise and eject the borrower (who has given no consideration) at will.[79] In cases of hire, on the other hand, the hirer would be protected by the implied warranty as to quiet possession.[80] A similar result (though not, in this case, reinforced by statute)[81] would appear to follow where the bailment is contractual but not one of hire.

Again, the borrower's security of tenure is rarely the subject of express provision outside the United States. Museum officials appear to accept that a lender who calls for the premature return of the object will get it, but should not count on the borrower's generosity or sympathy in later dealings. Claims for wasted expenditure are seldom if ever pursued.[82]

Duty to exhibit

A related issue is the right of exhibition. Some borrowing museums[83] explicitly disclaim all obligation to exhibit a borrowed work; display is expressed as a discretion in the borrower rather than a right of the lender.[84] The discretion is advisable, not least in regard to works of living artists, who may wish to adjust the number, quality and balance of works borrowed for exhibition, and may even invoke their moral right. Again, however, it requires no vivid imagination to predict the losses and other disappointments which lenders may suffer through a misplaced expectation that a work was to be exhibited. A lender who had been contemplating sale or a further lucrative loan after the successful conclusion of the current loan may threaten to sue for damages for loss of opportunity.

Such a claim raises two main issues: the existence of the obligation and the damages payable for its breach. There is no authority on the first point. If the loan is a contract, the lender may argue that efficacy[85] requires a term to be implied that the borrower will exhibit the object, subject only to those supervening events[86] which frustrate the contract. The borrower may counter, however, by arguing (i) that a duty to exhibit is unnecessary to the efficacy of the loan, perhaps because the loan confers on the lender other benefits which do not depend on exhibition, and (ii) that the written terms of the loan are an exhaustive statement of the parties' duties, leaving no room for an implied obligation to exhibit.[87] If the loan is not a contract, the lender must try to establish a duty in tort, or by virtue of the distinct relationship of gratuitous bailment. Liability in tort or bailment may certainly arise where the non-exhibition of the object stems (say) from its negligent damage by the borrower, but liability for mere omission (such as a simple failure to exhibit) is far more contentious. All that can be said with confidence is that a positive promise to exhibit should be enforceable, even under what would otherwise be a simple loan.[88] In that case, each party is contributing to the bargain: the borrower gets possession and the lender gets the exhibition. In short, the loan becomes a contract.

Once the duty is established, one must quantify the lender's recoverable loss. In such a case, the conceptual identity of the loan again becomes crucial. If the loan agreement is a contract (whether of hire or otherwise) damages for loss of opportunity are in principle recoverable in an action for breach,[89] subject to requirements of foreseeability, causation and remoteness. If the loan is not a contract, and can be enforced only by an action in tort, the position is much less certain. The lender may well be defeated by authorities which indicate that tort law does not lend itself to the recovery of expectation[90] or opportunity losses.[91]

What, then, if the lender asserts an independent claim for breach of bailment; does liability follow contract or tort, or does it strike a path of its own? Perhaps unsurprisingly, there is no authority on this issue.

Scarcely less impenetrable are the legal issues which can arise where a private lender sues not for defeated economic expectations but for personal disappointment, distress and inconvenience caused by the borrower's failure to exhibit.[92] One hears of lenders who (sometimes accompanied by friends) traverse continents to view a favoured work on display, only to find that is has been relegated to the basement. Such cases are believed to have precipitated some of the express United States provisions on borrower's discretion. And yet the majority of English standard loan agreements continue to leave this issue unaddressed. Here, as elsewhere, those officials who have considered the matter appear confident of an amicable resolution.

Authenticity and attribution

A further area where it can be important to distinguish contract from tort is authenticity. To a lawyer, the potential liability of a lender for the inauthenticity of the loaned object is to be taken seriously. Adverse consequences akin to those arising on a judicial seizure or premature withdrawal of the work[93] may afflict the borrower who discovers that a borrowed work is inauthentic.

The ability of such a borrower to recover damages from the lender may be enhanced if the loan agreement can be classed as a contract of hire. Strict liability terms may then be implied by statute, to the effect that the object corresponds with any description or sample, is reasonably fit for its purpose and is of satisfactory quality.[94] Admittedly that does not guarantee recovery, not least because the court may hold that the borrower relied on its own judgment in verifying the picture,[95] or that the lender expressly or impliedly disavowed any guarantee of authenticity.[96] But the borrower's position is appreciably weaker where the foundation for the claim is a simple loan bailment unaccompanied by contract. In that event, there is a descending scale of possibilities. At best, the lender may owe the borrower a duty of care.[97] Failing that, a court may characterise the inauthenticity of the work as a "defect" and apply the "known" defects rule;[98] such an approach would make the lender's liability scarcely higher than that for fraud. Finally, and perhaps most probably, the court may reject the claim on the ground that it is without precedent, unsustainable for lack of intent to create legal relations, and a bald device to paper over the inefficacy of the transaction as a contract.

This seems to be another area where disappointed borrowers seek their consolation outside the law. Many curators take the view that, since the borrower institution is likely to have as much expertise as the lender, errors must be put down to experience: the borrower, having done the necessary research, takes the risk.[99] Beyond a possible exception where a lender has deliberately deceived the borrower, legal action simply is not contemplated and standard loan agreements do not address the issue. With private lenders, diplomacy and wider self-interest are also powerful restraints. One may, perhaps, be forgiven for suspecting that amour propre also plays some part in this approach.

Choice of governing law

Controversy can also arise from the need to identify the system of law which governs a cross-border loan. Here again, the result may differ according to the legal nature of the transaction.

Where the agreement is a contract, the parties can agree both a governing system of law and a forum for adjudicating differences.[100] The selection may be express or implied and, subject to certain murky limits,[101] is binding even where the chosen system is otherwise unconnected with the agreement. A similar autonomy probably exists under consensual arrangements which do not qualify as contracts, such as true gratuitous loans.

In practice, as already suggested,[102] the managers of art loans often prefer to leave the choice of law open. Outside Federal countries,[103] express clauses are uncommon; one rarely encounters a space for them on the form.[104] Officials hint at cases where the urge to stifle potential disagreement is so strong that the parties produce two different choices in two separate documents (one emanating from each side) each purporting to be the governing law.[105]

Failure to state a governing law raises the obvious question as to how else that law may be identified. The question is primarily one for the conflict of laws rules of the forum. Few museum administrators are versed in such principles, and until proceedings are issued the forum may itself be in doubt. If the loan is a contract, an implied or constructive choice of law may be collected from the Rome Convention, where that applies, or under common law principles of the conflict of laws.[106] Failing that, the governing law will be the legal system with which the loan contract is most substantially and intimately connected.[107] Even lawyers find this test easier to expound than to implement.

The complications do not end there. A contractual loan, whose contractually applicable law is readily identified under these principles, may give rise to other (non-contractual) causes of action, so that the contractual choice may not be the only applicable system. A different choice from that indicated by the rules of contract may become necessary if, for example, the overseas lender brings an action in tort or for breach of bailment. There is a marked dearth of authority as to whether the system of law governing a gratuitous bailment follows that for contract or that for tort, or is independent of both.[108] If the applicable system is that dictated by the law of tort, the parties may have to decide whether the legal system indicated by the "double barrelled" rule in *Phillips v Eyre*[109] defers to some other system more substantially connected with the action.[110]

Further complexity may result from the fact that the loan may attract two choice of law rules: one for the consensual or personal aspects, and another for the real or proprietary aspects.[111] The legal systems indicated by an application of the contract and property choice of law rules may differ in given cases: contract is conventionally governed by the proper law,[112] property in moveables is governed by the *lex situs*.[113] The problem can arise under any cross-border transaction in portable wealth, but can be particularly acute in relation to art and antiquities.

The issues are no easier to solve if the bailment, being a simple gratuitous loan, is not simultaneously a contract. There seems, for example, to be no authority on the choice of law governing an action to enforce a gratuitous bailment,[114] or on the legal system which determines whether a borrower gets a proprietary interest or an enforceable term.

The reluctance of some museums to agree or state a governing law may reflect a more general trait, already noted. In some quarters, museum bailments are characterised by optimism and forms; by a conviction that to get the loan paperwork "in order" is more important than to inventorise its legal content. This is unobjectionable so long as nothing goes wrong. One would be hard put, however, to credit it with being the reason why nothing goes wrong.

Further incentives to art loans: should lawyers interfere?

Four factors seem most likely to influence a decision to lend: the availability of the work and the competing demands on it; its fitness to travel and the physical perils confronting it; the availability of a suitable indemnity or other economic safeguard; and immunity from judicial seizure or other legal entanglement at the instance of a rival claimant. While some of these concerns are clearly beyond the reach of law, others are an appropriate subject for legislative or contractual reform.

Some reforms could be implemented only by governmental action. Statutory guarantees against the court seizure of loaned objects offer an obvious incentive to lending,[115] but outside the United States they are rare.[116] In part, their rarity may stem from legal and political misgivings. Aside from general issues of constitutionality and human rights, a block on civil restitution could offend existing treaty obligations by which states undertake the cross-border return of unlawfully-removed cultural property.[117] If immunity from seizure is desirable, it may be better approached by international agreement than by unilateral local initiative.

Some museum administrators (and private collectors) are keen to see a proliferation and uniformisation of national indemnity schemes. Some also advocate a closer co-ordination of State indemnities and lenders' insurances. It is understood, for example, that loans to the United Kingdom from the United States have in the past raised questions as to whether the exceptions and conditions precedent of the United Kingdom indemnity unacceptably expose the lender to risks[118] which would not have arisen but for the loan. While these questions are now settled,[119] further rationalisation of the relationship between indemnity and insurance might usefully be explored.

Some institutions favour the exploration of a more general doctrinal alignment. In response to an international survey, many museums said that national laws governing loans (at least within Europe) might profit from a harmonisation which standardised every aspect of the transaction from liability for theft and damage to title warranties and rights of exhibition. The view was notable among German museums.

Beyond that, the provision of fiscal incentives to lenders might be worth exploring. Outside Germany,[120] few countries offer tax advantages to straightforward lenders of art.[121] At an international level, such advantages appear non-existent. It is tempting to believe that private collectors might lend more readily if the loan attracted some form of fiscal credit, but the prospect of serious cross-border tax initiatives seems remote.

At a contractual level, there are signs of a desire among museum administrators for greater textual uniformity. There is support for a measure of standardisation among loan agreements.[122] Even if absolute uniformity is impracticable, it may make sense to develop "library" clauses for use in recurrent cases. There is a tendency to re-invent the wheel, which might abate if lawyers and museum officials could devise a repertoire of terms. Of course, the use of standard clauses must be approached with caution. Drafters must bear in mind that a contract is a coherent and co-ordinated whole, not an eclectic scrapbook of randomly interchangeable terms.

The question remains as to the value of legal analysis to the administration of art loans. With respect to those whose experience persuades them otherwise, it is submitted that a modicum of soul-searching might be good for lenders and borrowers. Lawyers, for all their faults, ask questions, with an inquisitiveness often laced with pessimism. To read the standard loan forms of most museums is to bring such questions forth in volume. Some of them have been outlined: what, for example, should happen if the picture is exposed as a fake during the exhibition; what if the object is claimed by a third party; has the lender thought to provide for the temptations which might persuade him to withdraw the object during the loan, or the events which may induce the museum not to exhibit it; why have the parties included no term as to the disposal of the work after the exhibition, or left blank the box marked 'choice of law'; and what is the effect of silence on these and other points? To explain one's aims to students of another discipline can be to clarify those aims immeasurably. To understand what is legally feasible can be an important step in their attainment.[123]

Notes

1. See the discussion below of Governmental Indemnity Schemes, designed to cover works of art on loan to institutions in the indemnifying State, and of anti-seizure statutes, designed to immunise from judicial process works of art which are on loan to the particular country from abroad. The United Kingdon subscribes to the first of these initiatives but not to the second. In some countries, the management of art loans is also underpinned by the existence of special contracting and administering bodies. One example, from Australia, is Art Exhibitions Australia Ltd, a Federally-funded company limited by guarantee which acts as a contractual funnel for exhibitions into Australia from plural lenders. Similar organisations, privately owned and founded on a commercial basis, exist in the United States and elsewhere. A further example is the Trust for Museum Exhibitions, which contracted as principal with the Greek Government to hold the Greek Gold exhibition in England.

2. Such counsel are employed by the more affluent museums in the USA, but are by no means typical even there. Beyond the USA, they are very rare animals.

3. In that the act of one party, the lender, is unrewarded; the benefit accrues solely to the borower.

4. In fact, most bailments of art by way of "loan" appear to be beneficial to both parties, but this fact seems not to be fully appreciated: see further below.

5. *Walker v Watson* [1974] 2 N.Z.L.R. 175.

6. In the ensuing account, the word "museum" is to connote both museums and art galleries; no distinction is intended between the two.

7.   These observations apply primarily to pre-loan negotiation and drafting. Many museums have stated, in response to a survey, that they readily seek legal advice if difficulties (e.g., theft, damage, disputed condition) arise in the course of an existing loan. In addition, larger loan agreements involving special legal, diplomatic or economic considerations are almost invariably negotiated and drafted by lawyers, particularly where governments are involved. An important example is the loan of the Thyssen-Bornemisza Collection to the Villa Hermosa at Madrid, a loan which has since been succeeded by the transfer of full title.

8.   These standard conditions may, of course, be adapted according to circumstance. One of the difficulties of this may be partial emendation which does not pursue and accommodate the repercussions of the particular revision within the agreement as a whole.

9.   Of course, those institutions which can afford in-house counsel, or which have qualified lawyers as Directors, are able to keep their procedures and standard agreements under regular review. But such appointments are rare outside the larger United States museums.

10.   See further below.

11.   A related problem may be the general unfamiliarity of practising lawyers with the conventions and objectives of the art world. In the words of one curator, "Solicitors have little to offer us as they have little expertise in this field apart from advising on specific points of law."

12.   Art loans interact with title disputes at two main levels. First, an art loan may be negotiated as a substitute for full proprietary restitution. That formed the basis of negotiations for the return of the Sphinx's beard, which the British Museum had contemplated returning to Egypt nearly a decade ago. Secondly, an art loan may arise as a consequence of proprietary restitution: a collateral transaction to mollify the dispossesed party. Such, it appears, was the position with some of the returns of Mayan objects to Mexico by United States Museums. The entrustment of a sacred object to a responsible museum may be an appropriate way of honouring it, and of sharing custody between spiritual and temporal guardians, without offending the object's essential sanctity. An example is the agreement reached between the Saanich People and the Archaeology Department of the Museum of Archaeology and Anthropology at the Simon Fraser University, British Columbia, regarding the entrustment of the Newtown Cross Roads Stone Bowl.

13.   It is understood, for example, that the recent tour of the Barnes collection of Impressionist paintings attracted loan payments in excess of $10 million.

14.   These were clearly among the factors motivating the recent loan of the Barnes collection to Paris and Tokyo, and are especially attractive considerations in the case of long-term loans.

15.   For example, the Guggenheim Museum's in-loan terms.

16. Viz., "we'll cross that bridge when we come to it".
17. (1703) 2 Lord Raym 909. For a modern discussion of the legal attributes of chattel loans, see Palmer, *Bailment* (2nd ed, 1991) Chapter 11.
18. See also *Blakemore v Bristol & Exeter Ry* (1858) 8 E & B 1035. Of course, "contract" means different things to different legal generations. Even so, nostalgia for a contractual analysis, or at least for the view that gratuitous bailments in general are honorary members of the contractual family, has been manifested as recently as 1974: see *New Zealand Shipping Co Ltd v A N Satterthwaite & Co Ltd, The Eurymedon* [1975] A.C. 154 at p. 167, per Lord Wilberforce.
19. *Exactissima diligentia*, or the avoidance of slight neglect.
20. Where the common law duty was (and is) one of reasonable care.
21. *Coughlin v Gillison* [1899] 1 Q.B. 145.
22. *Biddle v Bond* (1865) 6 B. & S. 225. See generally Palmer, op. cit., 265-86.
23. Favoured by general law, but never explicitly applied to loan bailments.
24. *The Winkfield* [1902] P. 42; *O'Sullivan v Williams* [1992] 2 All E.R. 385; Palmer, *Bailment* (2nd ed, 1991) Chapter 4.
25. *The Winkfield*, above.
26. *Walker v Watson* [1974] 2 N.Z.L.R. 175.
27. *Walker v Watson*, above: Palmer, op. cit., Chapter 9; but c.f. *The Eurymedon*, above.
28. *Mitchell v Ealing London Borough Council* [1979] Q.B. 1; *Houghland v R R Low (Luxury Coaches) Ltd* [1962] 1 Q.B. 694; *Griffiths v Arch Engineering Ltd* [1968] 3 All E.R. 217.
29. Above.
30. Viz., those situations where the circumstances surrounding an original deposit of a cultural object with a museum have become forgotten and the nature and effects of the transaction are no longer discoverable.
31. See generally Palmer, op. cit., Chapter, 1, 9, 11.
32. Analysed in Palmer, op. cit., Chapter 19.
33. See below.
34. Below.
35. See further below.
36. *Dollar v Greenfield* The Times, 19 May 1905.
37. *Travers & Sons Ltd v Cooper* [1915] 1 K.B. 73.
38. Other possible consequences of the contractual classification are examined below.
39. In common with his analysis of the law of bailment generally.
40. In some common law countries, the Roman influence appears to survive. Less than twenty years ago Zelling J. of the Supreme Court of South Australia consulted the *Lex Aquilia* in determining the liability owed by the lender of a dangerous onion sorting machine to a third party who was injured during use: *Pivovaroff v Chernabaeff* (1978) 21 S.A.S.R. 1.

41. These include loans by private individuals to public bodies.

42. Loans from Greek museums are characteristically the product of agreement between the Government of Greece and the borrowing institution. An example is the agreement between Greece and the Trust for Museum Exhibitions in respect of the Greek Gold exhibition. The Trust was acting as agent for a stated set of borrowers.

43. The Paris Convention on International Exhibitions (1928) is inapplicable to fine art loans: Article 1(1). The UNESCO Declaration on the International Exchange of Cultural Property (Nairobi, 1976) contains little that is directly applicable to loans. The Declaration is largely aspirational and appears primarily to contemplate the making of outright dispositions of cultural objects (eg, gifts, sales, or exchanges in the literal sense) among States or national cultural institutions. Interestingly, however, it recommends tax incentives to facilitate cultural propagation: c.f. below. The commonest form of generalised treatment is probably to be found in the codes of practice of the various museums' associations (for example, the ICOM and Museums' Association Codes) although these have little if any legal force. As to the ambiguous and apparently ineffectual nature of the provisions of the United Kingdom Museums' Association Code of Practice regarding loans, see Palmer, *Recovering Stolen Art* (1994) 47 *Current Legal Problems* pp. 226, 240-50, especially at p. 245.

44. See further below.

45. As, for example, in the case of "Agreed Condition Reports".

46. *Lilley v Doubleday* (1881) 7 Q.B.D. 510; Palmer, op. cit., pp. 670-4, 834-40, 1270-5.

47. See, for example, the Getty, Guggenheim and Hirschhorn standard terms for incoming terms. Similar observations apply to Canadian and Australian museums, whose standard forms draw heavily on United States models.

48. Such as a depositary or mandatary.

49. *Doorman v Jenkins* (1834) 2 Ad. & E. 256; c.f. *Morris v C W Martin & Sons Ltd* [1966] 1 Q.B. 716 at 725, per Lord Denning MR; Palmer, op. cit., 546.

50. As the borrower acts towards its own property.

51. Sections 2 and 3 of the Act would appear to be applicable, the latter depending on whether the loan is a contract. Where the loan is a contract and the lender is a "consumer" within Regulation 2(1), the terms of the loan may also be rendered ineffective on the ground of unfairness by the Unfair Terms in Consumer Contracts Regulations 1994, SI 1994 No. 3159. For that conclusion to follow, however, the transaction must be a contract for the supply of services by the borrowing institution (acting for purposes relating to its business) to the lender: Regulation 2(1). The Regulations apply, within limits, to all contract terms and not merely to

exclusion, limitation and indemnity clauses.

52. Section 11(5) Unfair Contract Terms Act 1977. In contrast, the burden of proving the unfairness of a particular contract term appears to rest on the consumer under the Unfair Terms in Consumer Contracts Regulations, above.

53. Palmer, op. cit., pp. 779-824, pp. 1263-9.

54. Palmer, op. cit., pp. 665-70.

55. A typical example is the Museum of Modern Art loan form provision for insurance. Versions of the broad model outlined in the text are adopted by most, if not all, major United States museums.

56. Typically, loss or damage resulting from wear and tear, gradual deterioration, moths, vermin, inherent vice, war, hostilities, insurrection, nuclear reaction or radiation, and damage resulting from any unauthorised repairing, restoration or retouching process.

57. The Netherlands is currently in the process of revising its Indemnity Rule to cover a broader range of museums.

58. National Heritage Act 1980, s. 16.

59. Quaere whether such a contract might not, in the case of a private lender, attract the supervisory jurisdiction of the Unfair Terms in Consumer Contracts Act 1994, SI 1994 No. 3159, exposing the agreement to the assertion that it is ineffective on the ground of unfairness. This is not to suggest that the terms of the indemnity are in fact unfair. The Unfair Contract Terms Act 1977 is presumably inapplicable to the agreement by virtue of the statutory exclusion relating to contracts of insurance: see Schedule 1 para 1 of the Act. There is no such exclusion in the 1994 Regulations.

60. See below.

61. In a typical loan agreement, the lender permits the borrower to make photographic reproductions for catalogue and postcard sales. Royalties may be paid, but this is by no means standard.

62. These are, as may be expected, normally the responsibility of the borrower.

63. Neither borrowers nor lenders normally want a borrowing institution to get involved in repairing, onserving or cleaning a borrowed work, and typical clauses will ban this unless by consent of the owner. But the museum may reserve the right to treat the object in an emergency and to charge the owner for this.

64. That is, deposits of objects which occurred so long ago that the museum is either uncertain whether the objects were loaned or given, or unable to trace the lender or its descendants: see above. Certain States of the United States make legislative provision for such dilemmas: see, e.g., the Maine statute of 1981 (27 M.S.R.A. c19 para 601) and the California statute of 1983, set out in Malaro, *A Legal Primer on Managing Museum Collections* (1985) 195-203.

65. See, for example, the standard in-loan terms of the J. Paul Getty Museum.

66. For example, the out-loan terms of the National Technical Museum at Prague.

67. For example, the in-loan terms of the J. Paul Getty Museum.

68. See below.

69. This assumes that the loan is a contract; if the bailment is a truly gratuitous loan, the promise as to title would on a conventional analysis be unsupported by consideration. See further below.

70. *Tai Hing Cotton Mill Ltd v Liu Chong Hing Bank* [1986] A.C. 80; but c.f. now *Henderson v Merrett Syndicates Ltd* [1994] 3 All E.R. 506, H.L.

71. Supply of Goods and Services Act 1982, s. 7. The position is broadly similar under Australian, New Zealand, Canadian and United States Law.

72. See *Biddle v Bond*, above.

73. See *Campbell v O'Donnell* [1967] I.R. 226; Palmer, op. cit., pp. 631-54.

74. *Coughlin v Gillison*, above.

75. An exception is occasionally acknowledged where a lender has been fraudulent. The author has, however, spoken to no institution which admits to being a victim of fraud in this regard.

76. It is understood that "reciprocal loans" of this kind are occasionally made to private lenders by United States museums. They are less likely to occur in the United Kingdom, where heavy constraints govern the lending of objects from the National Museums and Galleries.

77. Palmer, op. cit., pp. 658-65.

78. It is not uncommon for museums to make express provision in their out-loan terms for withdrawal of the loaned object at their discretion: see, for example, clause 14 of the out-loan terms of the National Museum of Scotland.

79. There is an alternative view, which is that the lender is bound by the promise of a secure term (irrespective of conventional consideration) from the time the borrower, relying on this promise, takes possession: see Palmer, op. cit. supra.

80. Supply of Goods and Services Act, section 8.

81. Section 2 of the Supply of Goods and Services Act would not apply here because the transaction is not one for the transfer of (property in) goods: see ibid., s. 1.

82. A news report in The Daily Telegraph for June 14th 1995 recounts the withdrawal by the lender (a dealer) of Sir Francis Grant's picture "The Master of Dartmoor Hunt" from a exhibition at the Tate Gallery during that exhibition. It appears that no redress was sought by the gallery.

83. For example, the Getty Museum.

84. Note, however, that the lender may be mollified by a further term whereby, in the event of non-display, the borrower agrees to retain the work for the agreed time, so saving the lender the inconvenience of an early return.

85.   *B P Refinery (Westernport) Pty Ltd v Hastings Shire Council* (1977) 52 A.L.J.R. 20.

86.   Such as destruction of the museum: *Taylor v Caldwell* (1863) 3 B. & S. 826.

87.   See *Tai Hing Cotton Mill v Liu Chong Hing Bank* and c.f. *Henderson v Merrett Syndicates Ltd*, above.

88.   C.f. *A R Williams Machinery Ltd v Muttart Builders Supplies Winnipeg Ltd* (1961) 30 D.L.R. (2d) 339 (1961) 31 D.L.R. (2d) 187; Palmer, op. cit., pp. 666-8.

89.   *Chaplin v Hicks* [1911] 2 K.B. 786; and see *Obagi v Stanborough (Developments) Ltd* (1995) unreported, 7th April, C.A.

90.   C.f., however, *Ross v Caunters* [1980] Ch. 297.

91.   See generally *Hotson v East Berkshire Area Health Authority* [1987] A.C. 750; *Lawson v Lafferiere* (1991) 78 D.L.R. (4th) 609; c.f. *Poseidon Ltd v Adelaide Petroleum NL* (1994) 68 A.L.J.R. 313; *Hardware Services Ltd v Primac Association Ltd* [1988] 1 Q.d. R. 393; Lunney (1995) 15 *Legal Studies* 1.

92.   As to the restricted right of recovery for such losses under English law, see *Watts v Morrow* [1991] 4 All E.R. 937, C.A.; c.f. *Ruxley Electronics and Construction Ltd v Forsyth* [1995] 3 All E.R. 268, H.L.

93.   See above.

94.   Sections 8 to 10, Supply of Goods and Services Act 1982, as amended by the Sale and Supply of Goods Act 1994.

95.   That would, apparently, accord with the normal expectations of institutional borrowers: see the quotation set out at text adjacent to n.11 above.

96.   English decisions on the sale of works of art show a judicial reluctance to adjudicate upon matters of authorship or to conclude that sellers gave affirmative undertakings on such matters: see *Harlingdon & Leinster Enterprises Ltd v Christopher Hull Fine Art Ltd* [1990] 1 All E.R. 737; *Leaf v International Galleries Ltd* [1950] 1 All E.R. 693; c.f. *Marie Zelinger de Balkany v Christie Manson & Woods Ltd* (1995) *The Independent* 19 January (Morison J); *May v Vincent* (1990) 10 Tr. L.R. 1, D.C.

97.   C.f. *Luxmoore-May v Messenger May Baverstock* [1990] 1 All E.R. 1067.

98.   *Coughlin v Gillison*, above.

99.   See the quotation set out above. C.f. the reasoning of the Court of Appeal in the *Harlingdon & Leinster* case, above.

100. European Union, Rome Convention on the Law Applicable to Contractual Obligations 1980, Art. 3, enacted into United Kingdom law by the Contracts (Applicable Law) Act 1990 Art. 3 (applicable to transactions concluded after April 1st 1991); *Vita Food Products Inc v Unus Shipping Co Ltd* [1939] A.C. 277 at 290 per Lord Wright (pre-existing common law).

101. Ibid.

102. Above.

103. Notably, the USA, Canada and Australia.

104. Specifications as to governing law are altogether commoner in the case of State indemnities for loans of art works. It is conventional for the Indemnity Deed or other instrument to specify the law of the country affording the indemnity as that governing its interpretation and validity. That is, for example, the position under the United Kingdom Indemnity Scheme and the Dutch Indemnity Rule. It is understood that the binding effect of such clauses has occasionally (albeit informally) been questioned.

105. A similar reticence seems to apply to other aspects of the machinery of dispute resolution. It is also rare among European museums to find exclusive jurisdiction clauses and arbitration clauses in loan agreements.

106. See the *Vita Foods* case, above.

107. Rome Convention 1980, above, Art. 4 (contracts made after April 1st 1991); *Bonython v Commonwealth of Australia* [1951] A.C. 201 at 209 per Lord Simonds (common law).

108. C.f. Palmer, op. cit., pp. 71-4.

109. (1870) L.R. 6 Q.B. 1.

110. *Boys v Chaplin* [1971] A.C. 356; *Red Sea Insurance Co Ltd v Bouygues SA* [1994] 3 All E.R. 749. And see now the Private International Law (Miscellaneous Provisions) Bill 1994, Part III.

111. A distinct system of applicable law would certainly be appropriate to claims involving the proprietary position of third parties; for example, whether a borrower has conferred title to the goods on a bona fide purchaser.

112. Above.

113. That is, the law of the country where the object is located at the time of the transaction in question: *Cammell v Sewell* (1860) 5 H. & N. 728; *Winkworth v Christie Manson & Woods Ltd* [1980] Ch. 496.

114. C.f. Palmer, op. cit., pp. 71-4.

115. A distinguished private collector, responding to a survey, has described such legislation as essential, particularly in the fields of archaeology and ethnography. This view is supported by a prominent New York gallery counsel whom the author interviewed.

116. See Federal Act 22 USC para 2549, Immunity from Seizure Statute. New York has independent legislation immunising art loans from judicial seizure: N.Y. Arts & Cult Aff Law. The statutes are briefly compared by Lerner and Bresler, *Art Law* (1989) pp. 102-3. Anti-seizure legislation also exists in four Canadian provinces, viz Ontario (Foreign Cultural Objects Immunity from Seizure Act), Quebec (Art 553.1, Code of Civil Procedure), British Columbia (Law and Equity Act 1980, RSBCC 224) and Manitoba. In 1994 France legislated to immunise certain specified

overseas art loans from seizure for the period of the loan in France, where the exhibition and the individual works loaned are designated by ministerial order: loi no 94-679 of 8 August 1994, Art. 61. Since the 1994 law came into force, orders have been made in relation to exhibitions of works by Maurice Denis (21 September 1994) and Andre Derain (28 September 1994). The legislation followed Irina Shchukina's unsuccessful action in Paris in 1993 to recover certain works by Matisse, which had been owned by her father and taken into state ownership by the Soviet Union in 1918. The author is indebted to Sosthene de Vilmorin, advocat, Paris, for this information. As to the Shchukina litigation, see Boguslavskij (1995) 4 *International Journal of Cultural Property* 325.

117. As imposed, for example, by the 1993 EU Directive on the Return of Cultural Objects Illegally Removed from the Territory of a Member State No 93/7/EEC (OJ No L74/74, 27th March 1993), enacted into English law by the Return of Cultural Objects Regulations 1994 SI No. 501 of 1994 (Palmer, *Recovering Stolen Art* (1994) 47 C.L.P. 215 at pp. 228-30, 237-9) and by the Protocol to the 1954 Hague Convention on Protection of Cultural Property in the Event of Armed Conflict (see also Article 4(3) to the Convention).

118. For example, responsibility for negligence of the lender's servants and agents.

119. Private information available to the author.

120. In Germany, a committed, five-year gratuitous loan to a German public museum attracts relief from wealth tax: Sec. 101 No. 5, 110(1) No. 12, Valuation Law. The author is indebted to Dr Anna-Dorothea Polzer, of Heuking Kuhn Kunz Wojtek, Frankfurt am Main, for this information.

121. In the United Kingdom, relief from capital taxes under the conditional exemption scheme may require the owner of a work of art, while retaining ownership, to make it available for public exhibition. That seems to be the nearest that United Kingdom law approaches to offering fiscal incentives for loans as such. In the United States, outright gifts or shared ownership schemes ("partial gifts") may attract relief but simple loans do not. See generally Lerner and Bresler, op. cit., pp. 601 et seq.

122. Again, standardisation seems to appeal particularly to, but is by no means restricted to, German museums,

123. This paper summarises certain conclusions reached from a survey of art loans by the author under the auspices of the International Bar Association Educational Trust between 1993 and 1995. The full text of the Report will be published as a monograph in 1995. The author gratefully acknowledges the guidance and support he has received from the Trust during this inquiry.

7 Implied Terms in the Employment Relationship

ROGER RIDEOUT

The Control of Bureaucracy

It is trite academic learning that the contract of employment operates in the hands of an employer as an instrument of servitude. Theoretically, it need not be that the employer controls its inception and initiates variation; but it is normally so in practice. The employee may, but rarely does, exercise his power to veto this initiative. Almost certainly without so intending, the legislature endorsed this process by the introduction of a statutory requirement for a written statement of the more frequently encountered terms; a statement prepared by the employer and usually pre-emptory of the employee veto.

But many contracts are even more extensively dominated by one party.[1] The applicant for a job has more chance of negotiating concessions than have the applicants for an insurance policy or a financial loan. What makes the employer initiative so significant in the manipulation of the contract of employment is revealed by Professor Hugh Collins[2] as the "bureaucratic" structure of the employment relationship. The contract defines the structure and entrenches it. It is the structure which provides a hierarchy of subordination. It would be difficult to accept, if we did not know it to be true, that the relationship of subordination depends essentially on the single implied duty to obey orders. The bureaucracy issues the orders, the contract turns them into a binding system of private law. Yet few would see the implied duty to obey orders as anything but an inevitable consequence of a relationship an essential characteristic of which - once seen as *the* essential characteristic - is the ultimate power of control. In other words, the duty to obey orders is as much a fact as the bureaucratic structure which makes use of it. Neither is an inherent product of the Creation. Perhaps academic communities were once communities of equals. The

119

committee structure which, twenty years ago, began to be regarded as a demonstration of inefficiency, was a remnant of this earlier avoidance of bureaucratic structure. Outside Oxford and Cambridge, that bureaucracy can be seen to have established itself. The truth of Collin's analysis is, it is submitted, plainly demonstrated.

The question must be posed of the means that exist, if any, for controlling this bureaucratic hierarchy in the interest of various subordinate strata. The most obvious, and most effective, means is by way of legislation, whether in codified or piecemeal form, but this exists only patchily in Britain. Legislation does appear, however, to be the chosen control mechanism of the European Union, against which it is probably unlikely that the United Kingdom will hold out. If legislative control expands other methods of control, such as the judicial use of the implied term examined in this article, will naturally become less significant. In the United Kingdom early statutory control was not unknown. The Truck Acts controlled methods of wage payment, whilst health and safety was controlled for 130 years by The Factories Acts. Both legislative systems originated early in the industrial revolution and became recognised exceptions to the general 19th century rule of laissez faire. Few have ever bothered to ask why. The reason may be competition among industrialists, the more important of whom saw such measures as a protection against the undercutting of standards by smaller competitors. Until the 1960s the accepted view of all political opinion in this country was that regulation of the employment relationship could normally be left to a balance of the forces of collective labour and collective capital. Very few exceptions apart from these early and well established fields were permitted to develop.[3]

Collective agreements might have exercised a controlling influence over the employment relationship as they do, to some extent, in France. Whatever criticism there may be of the method of reasoning in *Ford Motor Co. Ltd v. AUEFW*[4] it only endorsed a well-established expectation that collective standards should not override the individual contractual choice, but operate through it. If we are concerned with control of the relationship, however, we must distinguish between the typical British collective agreement, which deals with major economic elements, and other, less well known, forms which do actually control the relationship. Typical of these would once have been collectively agreed restrictive practices. These are plainly capable of exercising control over the bureaucracy of subordination, even if they are not part of the contract, by limiting managerial power of control. But the influence of such agreements has sharply declined not only in the UK but widely throughout industrialised countries. If the decline is neither terminal nor permanent it is certainly likely to be long term.

Collins suggests a third, hitherto unidentified, form of control through a sort of privatised form of judicial review. In his view, the relationship should be controlled externally by a requirement of reasonable conduct as the bureaucracy of the state is controlled by the criteria of judicial review. The logic of the equation of public standards in each of the two controlling bureaucracies is convincing and the proposition has the advantage possessed by few other critiques of a contractual basis[5] in that it does actually offer a formulated alternative. Nor can the alternative be said not to be viable, since it would constitute a step of degree, rather than principle, in France. In the United Kingdom, however, the step would be one of major principle. Any review of the short period in which the operation of judicial review over aspects of the employment relationship has been mooted in this country[6] suggests that such a development as Collins envisages is unlikely to arrive from what looks like an alarmed withdrawal to a narrowly defensible perimeter.

It is submitted, therefore, that one is left, in the foreseeable future, with the judicially implied term as the only significant means of controlling employer initiative in the formulation of the contract of employment. The potential effect that has had, and will have in future, to control the employment relationship and impose standards of reasonableness on its bureaucratic structure will form the basis of the remainder of this paper.

Business efficacy, officious intervention, policy and judicial discretion

Allegedly, as everyone knows, the justification for implication of a term into contract is the necessity of making the contract achieve its intended business effect. Alternatively the obviousness of the parties' intention has been put forward as a test.[7] Although the two tests obviously overlap they are also significantly different. It is, for instance, true that what is obvious is not always necessary. It is not intended to examine them in depth here because, it is submitted, they are as much a legal fiction as the man on the Clapham omnibus and the impartial purveyor of natural justice. The former is actually on the Bench, for no Judge is likely to decide that his conclusions are other than those of a reasonable man. The latter does not exist and the more we move away from those trained to recognise and suppress their own preconceptions the less protective value there is in this standard. So also, a search for the intention of the parties will reveal nothing. It took a surprisingly long time for the Court to admit that they would normally find no evidence of common intention[8] and they have not yet admitted that they will never find it. If there were evidence of common intention there would be evidence of agreement and thus of an express, albeit an oral, term. Equally, the necessity suggested by business efficacy depends on what it is thought the contract is intended to achieve. If efficiency is the driving motive, then, no doubt, one would agree that management must be free to dismiss those taking industrial action, the redundant, the inefficient and many another.

One would, like the common law, imply a right of termination by notice (preferably of short duration). But Socialist systems did not see productive efficiency as the only essential characteristic of the employment relationship. That may have been their undoing, but it remains true that the employment relationship could reasonably be seen as a means of providing men and women with the satisfaction of productive occupation, rather than the soul destroying frustration of idleness. In other words, even the individual right to terminate by notice is only essential if the contract is viewed with a particular objective in mind.

These are extreme examples so it is worth taking an actual situation and examining it in the light of supposed necessity. In *Gallagher v. The Post Office*[9] it was held that business efficacy did not require that there be a contractual obligation to recognise (that is, to bargain with) both of two designated trade unions either of which the employee was told he might join. The conditions in other jurisdictions, of course, might make such an obligation necessary but in the conditions prevailing then and now in Britain this might be seen as self-evidently correct. But if the question is looked at from the point of view of the employee, whose freedom to join one of two trade unions was acknowledged by the employer, there is a strong case for arguing that such a freedom is worthless in business terms unless the union he chooses can participate in bargaining. From that point of view, to give business efficacy to the acknowledgement, it must be necessary to accompany it by an equality of bargaining practice.

What this decision reveals most clearly, however, is a wholly unjustified objective approach to the contract in question.[10] And it is suggested that that discloses, equally clearly, the policy objectives pursued by the Court in this instance. It is true that many terms will be implied because they are characteristic of employment in general. Early text books on employment law contained chapters on the "rights and duties of master and servant" which were nothing more than a compendium of such generally applicable terms. No doubt, the mere fact of employment necessarily implies certain contractual terms. But the conclusion that no such *general* term is necessary cannot be the end of the enquiry into whether business efficacy or obvious needs demands *particular* implication into the contract in question. The question envisaged in *Shirlaw* is not seen as put to the reasonable employer and employee but to the parties to the particular contract; and rightly so. Employment is a diverse relationship in which that which is not necessary in most cases may be necessary in a particular instance. In fact, the point does not need to be strongly argued because very many judicial decisions accept this individual approach. The Court must, however, beware of turning the normal situation into a consistent policy. In *Gallagher*, therefore, the appropriate enquiry should have been whether acknowledgement of a policy of permitting employees to join one of two trade unions such as had occurred in that particular instance required, as a matter of business efficacy, that the two unions should have equal bargaining rights. It is, incidentally, probably true that this issue only arose obiter since neither the right to membership to one of two unions nor its consequential implication of bargaining rights would have been regarded as a matter to be incorporated into the contract of employment. That, however, does not alter the significance of the formulation of policy by generalisation.

122

For the same reason, care must be taken not to read generality into a decision that there is no implied term in a given situation. It may well be that the situation in question appears to be common. Even so, it would be dangerous to produce what looked like a universal rule because of that untested assumption. In *Laughton v. Bass*,[11] for instance, the conclusion that business efficacy does not demand the implication of a duty not to compete was presented by the Court as of general application. In the course of its judgement the Court explained the prohibition on spare time competition imposed in *Hivac Limited v. Park Royal Instruments Limited*[12] as derived from the need to protect trade secrets. But it seems likely that *Hivac* was decided on the assumption that implied duties should be of general application. If instead the particular circumstances of the employment relationship in that case are considered and especially precisely the need to protect vulnerable trade secrets, business efficacy might well have provided a justification for implied prohibition on competition in that contract and in others exhibiting similar characteristics.

Application of business efficacy to the contract in question, rather than to employment as a whole, might prompt a fresh look at a number of decisions in which it has been held not to support implications. It seems unlikely that there were special circumstances distinguishing *Lister v. Romford Ice and Cold Storage Company Limited*[13] from employment in general but there may well have been such circumstances in *Reid v. Rush and Tompkins Group.*[14] The policy reasons for not requiring all employers to warn all employees of unexpected economic risks when working in unfamiliar social and legal systems are obvious. But it would be a bold assumption that there are never circumstances justifying the implication of such a duty. If *Veness v. Dyson Bell & Co.*[15] had been viewed as one of a special relationship, as the same situation was in *Isle of Wight Tourist Board v. Coombes,*[16] business efficacy would surely have produced the same implied duty of politeness as was recognised in *Donovan v. Invicta Airways Limited.*[17]

The business efficacy test is much more likely to be infiltrated by policy considerations if it is seen as applying to employment relationships generally, but it is always prone to be influenced by unacknowledged assumptions about the proper nature of the relationship. The influence of policy, of course, is not confined to implied terms. To take only one example, the refusal to incorporate the terms of a collective agreement dealing with individual offers to redundant employees in the contracts of those employees[18] was openly said to depend on the assumption that managerial prerogative should not be fettered. No doubt, courts would react with disbelief to another suggestion that there should be an implied right to restrain a transfer of business.[19] But such situations could, and should, be dealt with on principle. It is difficult to infer a testy "Oh, of course!" on the part of management to a restriction on business transfer and business efficacy would seem to support its restriction, rather than otherwise. But courts which are increasingly recognising the need to offer reasonable protection to employees[20] should be prepared to question historic assumptions about their subordination to managerial power.

Once the test of business efficacy (or obvious need) has persuaded the court to imply a term it will very rarely be apparent what detail that term should contain. In *Howman and Son Limited v. Blyth*[21] Browne-Wilkinson J. (as he then was) appeared to regard contracts of employment as always likely to be of a type giving the courts discretion to imply detail on the basis of what was reasonable. He says:

> These implied terms may be of two types. The first (which we will call *The Moorcock* type) are terms which the parties, if they had been asked at the time of the contract whether the term was part of the contract would have immediately agreed that it was. The second type (which we will call "*The Lister* type") applies to cases, such as contracts of employment, where the relation between the parties requires that there should be some agreed term which has not in fact been agreed but both parties would not have agreed what that term would be if they had been asked. In the *Lister* type case, the court implies a reasonable term.

It is suggested that whether one imagines agreement between the parties or not it is difficult to imagine agreement in detail. In any event, as we have already said, agreement is only a matter of judicial inference. The courts are largely free to infer agreement to either generalised or detailed terms or to accept that there is no evidence of agreement and imply general or detailed terms as they see fit.

It is submitted, therefore, that the second stage of implication in which the actual term is formulated will require the application of judicial reasonableness. Whether the court is content with generalities or attempts to formulate detail will also tend to be a matter of its conclusions based on reasonableness. There is nothing new in *Mears v. Safecar Securities Limited*[22] save a relatively rare acknowledgement that this is so. Stephenson L.J. acknowledges that the statutory requirement for a written statement of selected terms and conditions would force the Court to invent such terms if there was no evidence of what the parties intended. But the same is rarely true if the pressure comes from the necessity of business efficacy. In such a case the court can stop at a generalisation if it so wishes.

This discretion has not always been apparent in the past and will not be so in the future in a high proportion of cases. We shall see, as this paper progresses, many examples of implication in general, and even ambiguous, language. Before the upsurge in demand for implied terms and a readily available judicial source of production the "rights and duties of master and servant" were usually of the general type. They survive today in much the same state. But the "newly discovered" implied duty to maintain trust and confidence is at least as lacking in particularity. When they discover an implied term of apparently general application the courts are, probably inevitably, inclined to formulate it only in general terms leaving it to comprehend particular fact situations as they arise.

The effort required of tailor-made detail is usually reserved for particular implication. But the application of a test of reasonableness is precisely the same whether the formulation is general or particular. Necessity, therefore, tells us that we need a term and nothing more. Reasonableness may be content to leave the expression of that term as general as "maintenance of trust and confidence".

The weakness of the implied term

The obvious weakness of any attempt to regulate contractual terms by the mechanism of contract is the existence of the veto which either party must be able to exercise over that external control. Hence, Professor Collins systems of private judicial review, which could declare such a veto unreasonable. The effect of the veto is seen at its clearest in the unilateral rejection of change which frustrates incorporation of collectively agreed terms. The courts have tacitly accepted a norm of incorporation which can probably be explained as endorsement of the expectation of management, employee and trade union.[23] Although this assumed incorporation appears to occur unless objection is expressed; and so, presumably, at the time of making the collective agreement, it can be frustrated by objection from one or other party before there is any evidence of acceptance by that party. Neither party has such an opportunity in the case of an implied term of which both will have been unaware until it is said already to exist. But the process of implication may be vetoed in advance by provision of an express term dealing with the area of necessity. Since, in practice, the employee is likely to agree the contract presented to him or her, this is effectively a unilateral veto on the power of judicial regulation. It is self-evidently logical that there can be no room for implication if the parties have expressly made provision and the rule that implication cannot override an express term is a statement of the inevitable. It is, nonetheless, a rule which can seriously damage the parties' expectation.[24] In the case of the implied term the express term contravening implication is likely to appear as a deliberate response by an employer to unwanted judicial regulation.

One of the clearest examples of such a response is the upsurge of activity devising generalised mobility clauses for express inclusion in contracts of employment most of which are designed to deal with the uncertain future conditions in which management may find of value the unilateral power to order the employee to move. Not always coincidentally, the operation of such a term will normally deprive an employee of a claim for compensation for redundancy, although there are signs of judicial willingness to challenge this consequence. The combined effect of decisions such as *O'Brien v. Associated Fire Alarms Limited*[25] and *Managers (Holborn) Limited v. Holme*[26] was to give the appearance of an implied term restricting the right to move the employee to an area within reasonable travelling distance of his home. Browne-Wilkinson J. in *Jones v. Associated Tunnelling Company Limited*[27] chose such a term even in the absence

125

of the indications from subsequent practice which existed in *O'Brien*. *Jones* was followed in *Courtaulds Northern Spinning Limited v. Sibson*[28] by a Court of Appeal anxious to point out that it implied the same term after careful consideration of the circumstances. It is apparent that the courts had come a long way from *Bouzourou v. Ottoman Bank* and *Ottoman Bank v. Chakarian*[29] when they sought to protect an employee by relying on a loose construction of the implied duty to obey reasonable orders (or perhaps orders lawful within the scope of the contract). It is also apparent that a particular implication of a wider mobility such as that derived from the provision, by collective agreement, of travelling and subsistence allowances in *Stevenson v. Teesside Bridge and Engineering Limited*[30] is likely to prove an uncertain power in management hands. It is entirely understandable that the employer, having had his attention so clearly drawn to the problem, should have responded with wide express terms such as that in *Rank Xerox Limited v. Churchill*[31] in which the duty was simply expressed to be a willingness to move.

There is sufficient authority now from which to infer that courts are not happy with so wide an obligation. In *Churchill's* case, exceptionally, it is suggested, the Court found it impossible to contemplate a situation in which the employer's power would vary as the employee changed her place of residence. Considering the fate of Browne-Wilkinson J.'s adventure in *Evans v. Elemeta Holdings Limited*[32] to introduce an element of reasonableness from the point of view of the employee into the normal business convenience which dominates unfair dismissal, it is too much to suppose that the Court might have accepted that one business purpose of the contract could be to permit the employee to earn a livelihood with reference to the practical pressure of ordinary life, so that if the employee had to put up with reasonable movement by the employer, so the employer should be regarded as required to accept that the employee might move home in the course of a working relationship. Nevertheless, Judge Hicks in the Employment Appeal Tribunal in *Bass Leisure v. Thomas*[33] simply swept aside the effect of the open-ended mobility clause in its relation to the critical area of redundancy compensation, holding that *UKAEA v. Claydon*[34] and *Sutcliffe v. Hawker Siddeley Aviation Limited*[35] were incorrect in accepting as a place of work an unascertainable area within which the employer had express contractual power to move the employee.

Other courts have revealed a certain ingenuity in avoiding the barrier erected by an express term to any qualifying implication. In *Bristol Garage (Brighton) Limited v. Lowen*[36] Arnold J. invented an unworkability which the successful operation of hundreds of similar contracts belies. An express term existed permitting the employer to deduct from the wages of a forecourt attendant till shortages arising from any cause. In the instant case the cause was third party dishonesty which must be one of the most normal reasons for till shortage. The Employment Appeal Tribunal concluded that no employee would have accepted employment on such a condition and business efficacy, therefore, requires qualification of the express term by the exclusion of liability for third party dishonesty. In fact, as everyone knows, a similar term was then common in the contract of forecourt attendants and it may be doubtful whether the practicable impossibility of discovering the intention of the parties, which has already been pointed out, should be exploited to assume an absence of intention to accept a commonly accepted term.

Apart from the fact that not all courts would agree that it is possible impliedly to qualify express terms[37] there is a logical argument that both versions of the test of implication are disabled by the express provision. If the parties obviously have considered the question and express their conclusion can they be required (or assumed) to think again? If, having thought, they express a conclusion, it might seem improbable that it is such that, without more, the contract is incapable of business efficacy.

An industrial tribunal in *Prestwick Circuits Limited v. McAndrew*[38] had adopted a similarly ingenious avoidance of the barrier, concluding that if there was necessity for a term to which the parties had responded by making express provision, business efficacy required that the term should operate reasonably. This is contrary to the decision of Wood J. in *White v. Reflecting Road Studs Limited*[39] that there could be no implication that express powers would be exercised reasonably; although he suggests that they should be exercised responsibly (which seems to mean, "for supportable reasons"). Even this possibility was rejected by the Court of Appeal in *Courtaulds Northern Spinning Limited v. Sibson*[40] where it was held that an *implied* power is not subject to an implied obligation to apply it reasonably, or even for genuine operational reasons.

The most effective challenge to an express term appears to be to confront it with an established requirement to the contrary. In *Johnstone v. Bloomsbury Health Authority*[41] slightly surprisingly, that requirement was the duty of care which exists, of course, as a general rule of law and an implied contractual term. Nevertheless, it is submitted that the impression given by the various judgments would support the view that a duty, however it arose, should remain unless the express term specifically contravened it. Browne-Wilkinson L.J. expressly said that an express term permitting 88 hours work per week would be enforceable notwithstanding the duty of care. Since it is as permissible to contract out of tortious liability as it is to displace contractual terms it is submitted that both should be sustained in face of all but a clear express provision to the contrary.

This would leave intact express provision where there was no pre-existing conflicting duty. In a case of the express mobility clause such as occurred in *Rank Xerox Limited v. Churchill*[42] for example, no other expression of mobility is to be found because there are no established details of such a contrary clause.

In *United Bank Limited v. Akhtar*[43] however, a means was found to qualify even a mobility clause. Fortunately for its potential it involves the implication for what may be described as fundamental contractual requirements. In that case the requirement was the duty to be available for work. There is no logical reason why it might not also be the need to maintain trust and confidence, so that the imposition of intolerable express provisions might be regarded as impliedly excluded. In *Akhtar* the contract contained an express, and almost unrestricted, power to require the employee to move anywhere in the country. When this was exercised, almost without notice and in a manner with which the employee could not comply, it was held that the application of an express right so as inevitably to frustrate the contract must be contrary to the business efficacy of that contract. The express term, therefore, required implied modification in order to prevent it destroying the efficacy of the contract. As the Employment Appeal Tribunal said, it must be obvious that all contracts contain an implied prohibition on frustration; so obvious that it is never expressed. That may be so, but it does not conclusively explain why the parties should not have expressly agreed that one of them can frustrate the contract; nor why non-frustration (or, for that matter, destruction of trust and confidence) must prevail over acceptance by the victim of a requirement with which as circumstances transpire he cannot comply. There is, after all, plenty of scope for the operation of the contract unless the frustrating power is invoked, and if it is, damages for breach of contract are payable.

The use of internal contractual regulation, by way of implied terms, to impose standards of reasonableness on the contract of employment is inevitably vulnerable to challenge by the parties who make the contract. The implied term is a useful weapon, partly because it cannot be countered by advance rejection. But it seems reasonable to say that it cannot withstand express exclusion. On the other hand, such express exclusion would have to envisage precisely those unforeseen situations which generalities in express terms are designed to embrace. It is in this area of interpretation of the scope of the express term that the implied qualification has room to operate. The crucial question is whether courts will lean in favour of treating the express term as all pervasive (as in *Rank Xerox Limited*), or as intended to be operated within reasonable bounds. At least, it would appear that the courts will not lightly permit their long established influence over the contract to be significantly eroded by an awakening employer awareness of what can be achieved by express provision.

The uncertainty of the implied term - the duty of trust and confidence

This paper has already commented on the marked uncertainty of the terms used to define implied terms of general application to employment. This point will now be illustrated by an extended reference to one in particular of those generally implied terms; namely the implied term that neither party to the contract of employment will act in such a way as to destroy the trust and confidence of the other necessary to sustain a working relationship. This term only emerged as such in the second half of the 1970s, apparently in response to a felt need to offer a remedy to an employee forced to leave employment by the intolerable conduct of the employer. There can be little doubt about the logical argument for such a term. However much it may be said that most contracts of employment do not involve considerable personal elements it cannot be denied that they do involve a personal trust and confidence. Indeed, in some nineteenth century cases, the test for a repudiatory breach was said to be one which destroyed the trust and confidence of the innocent party. Most law students, therefore, quickly conclude that this term is capable of being invoked in many instances where it is not easy to formulate any more precise provision. Its very uncertainty provides a ready-made precedent for new situations. What is not so often noticed is that the courts themselves adopt the same easy option on occasion, whilst academic commentators freely attribute this term to decisions which have no direct connection with it. It is submitted that it is not properly used as a compendium for a breach of other contractual terms which happen to be more difficult to formulate. It is normally used to reveal a breach of contract which strict examination of terms would not otherwise disclose.[44] In this sense therefore, it becomes an overriding provision. It is, perhaps, akin to recognition of a breakdown in the relationship. It would have very well described the situation which had developed in *Pepper v. Webb*.[45]

It has caused no surprise that rather meaningless general expressions of this type should be used to formulate a compendious provision capable of covering a wide range of associated activities. This, after all, is the same process in principle as the common law adopts when formulating a general rule of law from particular circumstances. Several of the generally applicable applied terms in the contract of employment, recognised before trust and confidence was added to their number, are of the same type. The duty of faithful service (even if expressed in its narrower form as "fidelity") is one of the most obvious examples capable of covering as divergent a set of circumstances as the use of confidential information acquired during employment, the making of a secret profit, and a duty to work normally.[46] It is even possible to include specific examples of a general principle under other general headings. The duty not to make a secret profit, for instance, might be included as part of fidelity or, alternatively as an aspect of the duty to account. Since we are concerned with the way in which these terms are expressed in practice it is no help to point out that a duty to account is more akin to a remedy than an implied term so that the implied term probably is fidelity, the duty to account rising from breach of that term. For the same reason, therefore, it is not surprising that the duty to maintain trust and confidence may be deduced from individual breach of other terms. It is of its nature capable of absorbing more particular expressions of obligation.

The vagueness of the expression may cause surprise despite a rather similar uncertainty in terms such as fidelity. Even more uncertain words have been used by courts in recent cases apparently to express very similar concepts. They include "loyalty"[47] "Goodwill"[48] "good faith"[49] and probably most uncertain of all being "good and considerate".[50] In the context in which it appeared in *Dalgleish v. Lothian*[51] even a so-called duty of confidentiality imposed upon the employer could be seen as a sub-division of the duty to maintain trust and confidence.

One may well ask, therefore, whether it is of any consequence that the Court should resort to such broad general expressions rather than more precise and specific formulations of implied terms. Does it matter, for instance, that the Court might speak either of the duty of an employer to support the employee's supervisory functions[52] or of a duty not to destroy trust and confidence? The significance of loose language, it is suggested, derives from the fact that the generalised terms are, in effect, rules of law applicable to the employment relationship. If one is to comprehend a number of specific terms within a broader category that category must be meaningful in itself. Otherwise, there is no certainty in the law governing the contents of the contract of employment. By saying that business efficacy demands the maintenance of trust and confidence the courts give themselves an unlimited discretion to incorporate any more specific term which can be brought under that general heading without necessarily considering whether that more detailed term is necessary in itself. To arrive at a position in which the overriding duty of the parties was to avoid making the contract unworkable would be to turn constructive dismissal into something akin to divorce. It would be a short step to recognise breakdown as the issue to be judged and that would be a plain acknowledgement that decisions were reached on the basis of impression. In other words, wide as is the discretion granted to courts by their own view of business efficacy, the test of necessity does impose an element of restriction which is not present in a concept of unreasonableness sufficient to cause a breakdown of the relationship. In this light, it is suggested, it would not be inconceivable that an employee should be able to claim that transfer of the business without consultation with him was intolerable.[53] Trust and confidence is, therefore, a dangerous concept unless it is carefully managed. The cases which we shall now consider reveal, it is submitted, anything but careful management. Not all the carelessness is attributable to the courts. Academic commentators are far too ready to bring within the list of cases illustrating this term decisions which have very little to do with this term save in the sense that it could be extended to absorb a more specific obligation upon which the decision was actually based.

The decision of Bristow J. in *Isle of Wight Tourist Board v. Coombes*[54] is often regarded as the earliest reported enforcement of a duty to maintain trust and confidence. It came in the midst of the dispute as to whether a constructive dismissal was a response to a repudiatory breach or unreasonable action.[55] Once that dispute has been resolved in favour of a breach of contract the industrial tribunals were induced to discovery of such breaches of contract in cases where their natural equitable instinct suggested that an employee had been treated in a way which should entitle him to leave his employment. *Coombes* made no attempt to establish a general duty. The Employment Appeal Tribunal said that the relationship between a director and his personal secretary must be one of complete confidence. *They* must trust and respect each other. There was also apparent in the case a distinct element of undermining the authority of the employee. The statement "she is an intolerable bitch on a Monday morning" was muttered to the Office Manager in the context of a dispute as to whether Mrs.

Coombes, or a more junior employee, should be doing certain typing. There is nothing to suggest the invention of a generally applicable term and the context of the case would have permitted any one of a number of much more specific of obligations to cover the situation. The same is true of the marginally earlier decision, also by Bristow J., in *Associated Tyre Specialists (Eastern) Limited v. Waterhouse*[56] when, clearly, the Employment Appeal Tribunal founded the constructive dismissal of Mrs. Waterhouse on the conclusion that when she was appointed a supervisor it then became a term in her contract "of fundamental importance" that she will have her employer's support providing she was acting in accordance with company policy. There is no mention in the decision of loss of trust and the court appears much more concerned to formulate a workable expression of the duty of support. In *Wigan Borough Council v. Davies*[57] the contract contained an express, albeit oral, duty of support but the Industrial Tribunal, for some reason, concluded that there was an implied term that the employer would provide reasonable support. It is probable that the tribunal was introducing one of the many confusions that befog this area by talking of implication as applying to the incorporation of an oral express term into the contract. Arnold J. in the Employment Appeal Tribunal made it clear that there would have been an implied term without such express incorporation. But let us suppose in this instance that the oral express term had modified whatever the implied term would have been. Since the courts tend to give no explanation of the content of the implied duty to maintain trust and confidence it would never be possible precisely to measure the extent of express modification. Folklore has it that the late Robert Maxwell once hired a personal assistant at an unusually high wage specifically to put up with being kicked around. Presumably, the express obligation to tolerate the otherwise intolerable would override the implication of a duty to maintain trust and confidence in that respect. Would this mean, however, that all aspects of trust and confidence were excluded and, if not, how would the courts decide which aspects were overridden by the express term?

If it is correct to see the courts, at this stage, as using the common law process of implication to develop a rule of law it is not surprising to find their early attempts to resemble a groping for the light. In *Fyfe and McGrouther Limited v. Byrne*[58] it is not entirely clear whether Lord McDonald, in the Scottish Employment Appeal Tribunal, meant to rely on the unreasonable loss of confidence by the employer or its consequent effect upon the employee's confidence in the employer. It will be remembered that the employer had, somewhat precipitately, called in the police, and alleged theft by the employee when elementary enquiry would have revealed that the transaction in question had been recorded by the employee, to the knowledge of his superior. The judgments of Lord McDonald were often regarded as conspicuous for their formulation of sensible rules, but in this instance he summarised his conclusion elliptically in the words, "They had indicated in the clearest terms that they no longer had any confidence in him or his honesty and that it is not unreasonable that by adopting this attitude in a situation for which he was not responsible they had destroyed any basis *of confidence in him or his honesty* that could ever exist between them and him in the future." Kilner Browne J. in *Robinson v. Crompton Parkinson Limited*[59] relied on *Fyffe* to formulate the wrong test. He said, "Thus an employee is entitled to say that there is conduct which amounts to a repudiation where the employer shows no confidence in him and has behaved in a way which is contrary to that mutual trust which ought to exist between master and servant...." Consequently where a man says of his employer, "I claim that you have broken your contract because you have clearly shown you have no confidence in me......" small wonder that the employer in *Courtaulds Northern Textiles Limited v. Andrew*[60] thought it a complete answer to assert continuing confidence in Andrew, blissfully unaware that they were, thereby, compounding the destruction of Andrew's trust and confidence in them. The judgment of Arnold J. contains what appears to be the earliest reported correct expression of a general duty:

> "The test must be....", he says, "that one implies into a contract of this sort such additional terms as are necessary to give it commercial and industrial validity. One of the ways in which it is put forward in the cross-notice by the solicitors for Mr. Andrew is to say that it was an implied term of the contract that the employers would not, without reasonable and proper cause, conduct themselves in a manner calculated or likely to destroy or seriously damage the relationship of confidence and trust between the parties."

This, however, does not indicate what conduct will suffice to destroy, or seriously damage, the relationship. *The Post Office v. Roberts*[61] stated only the obvious in holding that such conduct does not have to be deliberate or in bad faith. Ironically, that decision rejected the suggestion that it was sufficient if treatment was unreasonable on the ground that that was "too wide and uncertain". It is difficult to understand why unreasonable treatment should be uncertain when industrial tribunals are constantly having to judge that very issue in unfair dismissal cases. It is also significant that more specific implication is permitted to rest on a basis of reasonableness. In *White v. London Transport Executive*[62] Browne-Wilkinson J. held that there was an implied term obliging the employer to take reasonable steps to maintain appraisal during probation. If it is said that in this case the reasonableness was directed to sufficiently certain conduct then it may be pointed out that if maintenance of trust and confidence is sufficiently certain in itself the taking of reasonable steps to maintain trust and confidence must equally be sufficiently certain.

Objection to a criterion of reasonableness usually stems from a feeling that it nullifies the objection in *Western Excavating (EEC) v. Sharpe* to unreasonableness alone as a basis for constructive dismissal. So even Browne-Wilkinson J. was persuaded to refer to intolerable conduct in *Wadham Stringer Commercials (London) v. Brown*[63] whilst, possibly wisely, failing to indicate what implied terms the intolerable conduct broke. The same failure appears in the decision of Neill J. in *BBC v. Beckett*.[64] It is surely difficult in this latter incident to regard the employer's adherence to his contractual rights as intolerable, however unreasonable it may have been. The Court used neither term, but cannot have intended to suggest that there is an implied term that contractual powers will not be used unreasonably. Once again, superlatives like "grossly disproportionate" are meant to conceal the absence of any standard by which to judge the destructive effect.

The last word, to date, in the development of the implied duty to maintain trust and confidence was spoken in *Woods v. WM Car Services (Peterborough) Limited*.[65] Lord Wedderburn describes the decision of the Court of Appeal in this case as the most important judicial development of the 1980s. He describes the approach as "subjecting the employment contract to the employer's power to legislate at the workplace in order to improve the methods and the profits of "the business".[66] Up to that time the slowly emerging concept had seemed to operate in favour of the employee. Thereafter, it might be inferred that the managerial right to run the business properly could make even an employee's attempt to maintain her contractual rights unreasonable. The case seems to have raised strong feelings since Browne-Wilkinson J. came very close to re-assessing the facts found by the Tribunal. As Fox L.J. later pointed out, the Industrial Tribunal had found that the employer did not persist in its attempts to vary contractual terms and discussed proposed changes with the employee. The Employment Appeal Tribunal, however, described this situation as one in which the employer had persistently attempted to vary the terms, coming back after each withdrawal of one suggestion with a fresh requirement of a different kind, and that though it might not be fair to describe its conduct as unscrupulous it tried to reduce her wages, increase her hours, change her job title, fundamentally change her job content and impose a job description she considered more than she could manage. Clearly, if the courts are speaking of something as meaningless as sustained trust and confidence, the light in which undisputed facts are viewed will make a fundamental difference to a decision on the existence of a breach of contract. Yet it was Browne-Wilkinson J., no doubt deliberately, who laid down the clearest exposition yet of the implied duty to maintain trust and confidence; saying that there is an implied term that *employers* will not, without reasonable and proper cause, conduct themselves in a manner calculated, or likely, to destroy, or seriously damage the relationship of confidence and trust. He noted that intention was not essential to a breach and said that an Industrial Tribunal should look at the employer's conduct as a whole and determine whether it is such that its cumulative effect, judged reasonably and sensibly, is such that the employee cannot be expected to put up with it. Clear as this is, it seems to leave us with no better criteria than the Courts view of a reasonable employee's reaction to what is alleged to be intolerable conduct. This then, the newest of the generally applicable applied terms, is also the most extreme example of the courts assumption of complete discretion.

"Trust and confidence" has caught the public imagination as one might expect a slogan to do. In its heyday (which, incidentally, is passed not necessarily never to return) Industrial Tribunals frequently mentioned this as a ready help when no established implied term was in sight. It is difficult to explain to students why they should not do the same thing. If they may do the same thing when no other term is readily available why may they not adopt a similar policy when other more specific terms might serve the purpose. But more significant than that is the fact which we have observed that destruction of trust and confidence is capable of producing a breach of contract when all other terms of the contract have been observed. If Walton L.J. is to be believed[67] this may even be so where one party is "obdurately" refusing to agree to a variation of contract, as is surely her legal right. Not only does this implied term sweep the rest of the contract aside but it is capable of absorbing all its obligations (express and implied) in a single compendious concept. No other generally implied term has a precise meaning but it is submitted that they all use phrases which have some meaning. "Trust and confidence" relates to a state of mind which cannot be assessed. The gut feeling that the innocent party cannot be expected to put up with it is incapable of rationalisation. Nevertheless, arguing backwards, we are to believe that business efficacy requires a contract to contain a meaningless obligation. Equally, its total uncertainty does not render it unreasonable to imagine that the parties would have adopted it had they thought of it. Had a common law court been asked, in the abstract, to consider whether such a term was capable of implication it is suggested that it would have had no doubt of a negative answer.

The unpredictable effects of reliance upon this implied term may be demonstrated by comparison of the decisions of the Court of Appeal in *Bliss v. South East Thames Regional Health Authority*[68] and *Irani v. Southampton and South-West Hampshire Health Authority.*[69] It will be recollected that in the latter case an injunction was granted ordering the reinstatement of a consultant who had been requested to undergo a psychiatric examination for which the Court found no justification. The injunction was held to be correctly granted because the authority accepted that there was no basis for the allegations and, therefore, the trust and confidence remains. In the former case reference to an investigating panel, known in the Health Service as the "three wise men" had produced a finding that Bliss did not suffer from any pathological condition. Nevertheless, he was asked to undergo a medical examination and was suspended when he refused. Dillon L.J. described this as outrageous and a breach of duty to maintain trust and confidence. Assuming the two sets of facts can be equated on this point, it is then possible to waive the destruction of trust and confidence so that the innocent party can assert that he still retains it despite conduct which would, objectively, destroy it.

Power and complexity - confidentiality

It is evident from what has been said that use of the implied term confers on the courts the power to construct the contract of employment. In practice, in commercial contracts, the courts are reluctant to exercise the power of implication except in clear cases. In its application to the contract of employment the implied term assumes something of the character of medieval equity. There is plainly a tendency from an individual case to move towards the development of a general rule. But the analogy should not be pressed too far because it fails in two principle respects. The general rules that develop are by no means as certain as the rules of nineteenth century equity. Nor are they, it is suggested, the product of a desire to do individual justice. Commentators sometimes, rather loosely, express them as signs of the courts seeking to redress the effects of managerial prerogative. It is suggested, however, that there is no such general policy. If there is any guiding principle it is one of pure policy relating to employment as a whole. There is no doubt, however, that there is no longer any reluctance in the judicial approach to implication. It may have appeared at the time of the decision in *Lister v. Romford Ice and Cold Storage Company Limited*,[70] but there would be some hesitation to increase what was then, probably, seen as an established list of common law rules. If nothing else the pressure imposed by the need to satisfy the requirements of constructive dismissal would have eliminated such hesitation and *Gallagher v. TV Post Office*[71] may have been the last sign of reluctance. Subsequent decisions are more likely to be affected by specific policy considerations. Not surprisingly such policy may initially develop very slowly. Freedland suggested that there were signs of development in respect of the duty of disclosure of information as a result of the decision in *Sybron Corporation v. Rochem Limited*.[72] Up to this point courts had preferred to impose an obligation in particular cases by a wide interpretation of express provisions.[73] But *Horcal Limited v. Gatland*[74] in the same year, though considering the fiduciary duty of a company director, still hesitated to impose a duty on the individual where the value of the information was a matter of speculation. The prospect has plainly been opened. Policy considerations will dictate its future.

The considerable potential for the implementation of judicial policy which is thereby available can be demonstrated by one well known example; the withdrawal of the duty of confidentiality from a wide area of its previous application. The Report of the Law Commission on Breach of Confidence in 1981[75] states that the law of confidentiality has its foundations in equity. This is, to say the least, questionable. A line of eighteenth century decisions rested on protection of property whilst in the nineteenth century, the jurisdiction was initially founded in contract.[76] Excluding the unreliable authority of *Prince Albert v. Strange*[77] only *Gartside v. Outram* has a clear equitable base. Property, contract, bailment, trust, fiduciary relationship, good faith, and unjust enrichment have, at one time or another, been advanced as justification for judicial intervention with "the result that the answer to many fundamental claims remains speculative".[79] But the employment relationship has remained firmly based on an implied term of necessity in the contract of employment and predates, by many years, the systematic development of any equitable duty. The difference in effect of the two sources is plain in the decision in *Bents Brewery Limited v. Hogan*.[80] Nevertheless, the present writer, in 1983, suggested that contract and equity had arrived at very similar conclusions largely because the contractually implied duty would, in detail, be developed on a basis of reasonableness.[81]

It is no doubt natural, following the decision of the Court of Appeal in *Faccenda Chicken Limited v. Fowler*[82] for an increasing number of commentators to see the duty of confidentiality as an extension of the duty of fidelity. Obviously, "fidelity" is wide enough to comprehend confidentiality but, it is submitted, it has never done so up to the present time. The Court of Appeal, however, gave the impression that the strict duty extending to all confidential information during employment and imposed under the general heading of fidelity was modified after employment to become a duty in respect of a narrower range of information. There is no suggestion in earlier cases that this is how the duty of confidentiality was seen. Before *Faccenda* there is, it is submitted, no doubt that the duty of confidentiality as applied to the employment relationship extended to relatively trivial information.[83] Dispute as to the scope of its application centred around the distinction between information belonging to the employer and the assimilation of knowledge, converted into skill and experience, which could be said to belong to the employee.[84] There was no indication that any distinction would be drawn in employment which was not drawn elsewhere between "secrets" and information conveyed in confidence, despite the fact that the contractual duty relied upon in employment was almost invariably expressed as a duty to protect trade secrets. At the time the present writer suggested that this situation should hardly cause surprise. If the content of implied terms was determined by a test of reasonableness then it would seem natural that it should develop along much the same lines as the parallel rule in equity. Judicial thinking in earlier cases would not have been inclined to the view that the employee had rights which needed to be protected from the inhibiting effect of a very wide duty of confidentiality.

There is no doubt that the consequences of any attempt to distinguish between the employee's property and information and the property of the employer were likely to be uncertain and that if too much favour were shown towards employer ownership the marketability of the employee's skills was likely to be dangerously restricted. This is what the Court of Appeal concentrated on in *Faccenda Chicken Limited v. Fowler*.[85] The court's intention was plainly to produce a distinction based not on who owned the information but on its significance. It is submitted that no such distinction emerges in the rest of the law of confidentiality, whether it be based in equity or contract; and it had not previously existed in relation to employment. It is startling, but not surprising, that the Court of Appeal was forced to state that the employment relationship, alone, it would appear, among any situation in which information passes from one to another, was exempt from the operation of the equitable duty which its

136

decision indicated was thereafter, much more extensive. Indeed, the employment relationship, while it exists, would appear to be subject to a similarly strict duty of confidentiality as applies in equity to everyone else. Somewhat strangely, therefore, the former employee becomes exempt from the normal duty of confidentiality in respect of confidences he has enjoyed during employment. No doubt, the court felt able to introduce this limitation in view of the scope of the duty of fidelity operating during employment and capable of protecting all information derived during the existence of that relationship. As the decisions in *Roger Bullivant Limited v. Ellis*[86] and *Johnson v. Bloy (Holdings) Ltd and Wolstenholme Rink plc*[87] later revealed it is likely that the employer will be able to protect almost all tangible information, at least in the immediate aftermath of employment, so that the end effect is to free information in the mind of the employee for later use unless it represents a mental assimilation of significant trade related materials.

There are indications in the rather confused judgment of Goulding J., at first instance,[88] of a similar attempt to release the employee from too severe a restriction but there is no support for his dictum that trivial information cannot be regarded as confidential. Triviality is, in any event, an unworkable distinction since the only objective test would be the amount of damage likely to result from this disclosure. Triviality may serve to dispose of implied knowledge that the information was conveyed in confidence, but no more than that.

The Court of Appeal rightly distinguished between confidentiality and fidelity pointing out that the duty of confidentiality in employment had always rested on contract and had always been referred to as disclosure of trade secrets rather than protection of confidential information. It firmly took jurisdiction over the matter by stating that the content of the implied term was a question of law.[89] Presumably it is intended to indicate a greater degree of judicial intervention in implied terms. It thus prepares the way for a distinction between employment and all other relationships in which confidential information is passed from one to another.

The Court of Appeal relied heavily on remarks made by Cross J. in *Printers and Finishers Limited v. Holloway*[90] and the decision in *E. Worseley and Co. Limited v. Cooper*[91] to justify distinction between confidential information and trade secrets. Neither of these sources does provide such justification, however. Both rely on the well-recognised distinction between the employer's property in information and that of the employee in what he is carrying in his head. The Court suggested four criteria of the utmost imprecision by which to decide whether the information constitutes a trade secret or only some other form of information. It said, firstly, that the nature of the employment might give rise to higher obligations where confidential material is handled, because this would enable the employee to realise that the information was of a sensitive nature. Such realisation has always been essential for the equitable duty of confidentiality.[92] It may be questioned how either party, or the Court, will be assisted by detecting what is sensitive information if that is not an indicator of a trade secret. Nor is it very helpful to suggest that what may be a trade secret in the hands of one entrusted with it, is not so in the hands of a lower grade employee who comes across it accidentally. Secondly, the Court said that the creation of the material, which must be such as to require the protection afforded by a trade secret, would be a useful indicator. This appears to be a circular test. An attempt is made to explain the test by analogy with the excessive protection afforded by a restrictive covenant. This is rather more meaningful since it suggests that a trade secret is something of business value not available to others occupied in the same business, loss of which would be regarded as significant to the interest of the business. But cases on the validity of restrictive covenants rarely examine that aspect. The protection a restrictive covenant offers is likely to be sought as much because the employee has acquired information and personal skill *not* amounting to trade secrets. The question for a court is usually whether the protection against these acquired skills is too extensive, rather than whether protection is necessary at all.

The third criterion is said to be whether the employer has impressed confidentiality on the employee. But, again, it is difficult to understand how assertion of a duty which does not apply and which, if it did, would relate also to information less than trade secrets can be indicative of the existence of a trade secret. Finally, it is difficult to understand why the subjective view of the employer should indicate satisfaction of what is obviously intended to be an objective test. Fourthly, the Court of Appeal fell back on the very aspect of confidential information which had caused the problem of distinction, giving rise to concerns about policy by indicating an attempt to isolate information amounting to trade secrets from the employee's own knowledge. There never was any doubt that personal skills were not within the duty of confidentiality. Knowledge is another matter because it is usually a mixture of acquisition by trial and error, processes of observation and taught information. It is exactly how to sort out such information from the other sources and having done so to decide its significance which causes the problems.

In saying little more than that the implied duty of confidentiality should be confined to specific items of important information the Court of Appeal had driven back the boundaries of the duty spectacularly far. There is no doubt that after *Faccenda* the employee is much more free to sell his skills on the labour market than he was before. The Court had also taken control of the term since it had demonstrated that it cannot be defined within any boundary save that of reasonableness. However hard an individual employer might seek to protect specific items of information it is very doubtful whether he could reformulate the implied term in express form. Consequently, it would be impossible for an employer by express provision to exclude the courts from imposing the implied provision which rests largely on their own discretion.

There are other areas where, almost as significantly, the courts have demonstrated their power to alter the balance of the relationship between employer and employee by the introduction, or amendment, of an implied term.

A good example is the effect they have had upon the former right of an employee to be paid wages for partial performance of contractual obligations. Similarly, in that instance, the new implied terms are formulated as rules of law and it becomes difficult in practice to envisage the formulation of an express term which will exclude the implied term, save in relation to a particular foreseen event. In little more than twenty years the implied term in the contract of employment has developed into an instrument of judicial policy. It begins to look as if the courts have also found a way of preventing the frustration of that policy.

Notes

1. See Kahn-Freund, *A Note on Status and Contract in British Labour Law* (1967) 30 M.L.R. 635.
2. Collins, *Market Power, Bureaucratic Power, and the Contract of Employment* (1986) 15 I.L.J. 1.
3. One, of course, was the Disabled Persons (Employment) Act 1944, prompted, no doubt, by an anticipation of the aftermath of war.
4. [1969] 2 All E.R. 481.
5. E.g. Hepple, *Restructuring Employment Rights* (1986) 15 I.L.J. 69.
6. See e.g. Carty, *Aggrieved Public Sector Workers* (1991) 54 M.L.R. 129.
7. *The Moorcock* (1889) 14 P.D. 64. See also *Luxor (Eastbourne) Limited v. Cooper* [1941] A.C. 108 at 137. "What the law desires to effect by the implication is to give such business efficacy to the transaction as must have been intended at all events by both parties who are business men" per Bowen L.J. *Shirlaw v. Southern Foundries Ltd.* [1939] 2KB 206 at 227. "Prima facie that which in any contract is left to be implied and need not be expressed is something so obvious that it goes without saying; so that if, while the parties were making their bargain, an officious bystander were to suggest some express provision for it in their agreement, they would testily suppress him with a common 'Oh, of course'"; per MacKinnon L.J.
8. See *Jones v. Associated Tunnelling Company Limited* [1981] I.R.L.R. 477; *Mears v. Safecar Securities Limited* [1982] I.R.L.R. 183.
9. [1970] 3 All E.R. 712.
10. See, *Jones v. Associated Tunnelling Company Limited* [1981] I.R.L.R. 477 at para. 15.
11. [1986] I.R.L.R. 245.
12. [1946] Ch. 169. As, much earlier, had the present writer, Rideout, *Principles of Labour Law* (first Ed. 1972, Sweet & Maxwell Limited) at p. 89.
13. [1959] A.C. 555.
14. [1989] I.R.L.R. 65.

15.   *The Times* May 25, 1965.

16.   [1976] I.R.L.R. 413.

17.   [1969] 2 Lloyds Rep. 413.

18.   See *British Leyland Limited v. McQuilken* [1978] I.R.L.R. 245.

19.   *Newns v. British Airways plc* [1992] I.R.L.R. 575.

20.   See e.g. *Scally v. Southern Health and Social Services Board* [1991] I.R.L.R. 522.

21.   [1983] I.R.L.R. 139.

22.   [1982] I.R.L.R. 183.

23.   See Khan-Freund, *System of Industrial Relations in Great Britain*, ed. Flanders and Clegg (1954) pp. 58-9.   *Robertson v. British Gas Corporation* [1983] I.C.R. 353; *Marley v. Forward Trust Group Limited* [1986] I.R.L.R. 43.

24.   See e.g. *Gascol Communications Limited v. Mercer* [1974] I.C.R. 420.

25.   [1968] 1 W.L.R. 1916.

26.   [1977] I.R.L.R. 230.

27.   [1981] I.R.L.R. 477.

28.   [1988] I.R.L.R. 305. See also *Express Lift Company Limited v. Bowles* [1977] I.C.R. 474.

29.   [1940] A.C. 271 and 277.

30.   [1971] 1 All E.R. 296.

31.   [1988] I.R.L.R. 280.

32.   [1982] I.R.L.R. 143.

33.   [1994] I.R.L.R. 104.

34.   [1974] I.C.R. 128.

35.   [1973] I.C.R. 560.

36.   [1979] I.R.L.R. 86.

37.   See e.g. *Gascol Conversions Limited v. Mercer* [1974] I.C.R. 420; *Rank Xerox Limited v. Churchill*, supra.

38.   [1991] I.R.L.R. 191.

39.   [1991] I.R.L.R. 331.

40.   [1988] I.R.L.R. 305.

41.   [1991] I.R.L.R. 118.

42.   Supra.

43.   [1989] I.R.L.R. 507.

44.   See *BBC v. Beckett* [1983] I.R.L.R. 423.

45.   [1969] 1 W.L.R. 514.

46.   *Ticehurst v. British Telecommunications plc* [1992] I.R.L.R. 219.

47.   *Laughton v. Bapp* [1986] I.R.L.R. 245.

48.   *Ticehurst v. British Telecommunications plc*, supra.

49.   *Imperial Group Trusts v. Imperial Tobacco* [1991] I.R.L.R. 66; said in *Newns v. British Airways Corporation* [1992] I.R.L.R. 275 to mean "fair dealing".

50. *Woods v. WM Car Services (Peterborough) Limited* [1982] I.R.L.R. 413, per Denning M.R.

51. [1991] I.R.L.R. 66.

52. *Wigan Borough Council v. Davies* [1979] I.R.L.R. 127.

53. *Newns v. British Airways Corporation* [1992] I.R.L.R. 575.

54. [1976] I.R.L.R. 413.

55. The resolution of this dispute occurred in *Western Excavating (ECC) Limited v. Sharp* [1978] I.C.R. 205. "............in our judgment, the answer can only be, entitled according to law, and it is to the law of contract that you have to look."

56. [1976] I.R.L.R. 386. See also *Weatherall (Bond Street) Limited v. Lynn* [1977] I.R.L.R. 333.

57. [1979] I.R.L.R. 127.

58. [1977] I.R.L.R. 29.

59. [1978] I.R.L.R. 61.

60. [1979] I.R.L.R. 84.

61. [1980] I.R.L.R. 347.

62. [1981] I.R.L.R. 261.

63. [1983] I.R.L.R. 46.

64. [1983] I.R.L.R. 43.

65. [1981] I.R.L.R. 417.

66. Wedderburn, *TV Worker and the Law* (3rd ed.).

67. *Woods v. WM Car Services Limited* [1982] I.R.L.R. 413.

68. [1985] I.R.L.R. 308.

69. [1985] I.R.L.R. 203.

70. [1957] A.C. 555.

71. [1973] All E.R. 712.

72. [1983] I.C.R. 801. See Freedland *High Trust; Pensions and the Contract of Employment* (1984) 13 I.L.J. 25.

73. E.G. *Swain v. West (Butchers) Limited* [1936] 3 All E.R. 261; *Bell v. Lever Bros. Limited* [1932] A.C. 161.

74. [1983] I.R.L.R. 459.

75. Cmnd. 8388.

76. *Abernethy v. Hutchinson* (1825) 3 L.J.C.H. 209; *Morison v. Moat* (1851) 9 Hare 241.

77. (1849) 1 MAC and G. 25.

78. (1856) 26 L.J. Ch. 113.

79. Gareth Jones, *Restitution of Benefits Obtained in Breach of Anothers Confidence* (1970) 86 L.Q.R. 463.

80. [1945] 2 All E.R. 570.

81. Rideout, *Principles of Labour Law* (4th ed.)

82. [1986] I.C.R. 297.

83.   *Under Water Welders and Repairers Limited v. Street and Longthorn* [1968] R.P.C. 498; *Cranleigh Precision Engineering Limited v. Bryant* [1965] 1 W.L.R. 1293.
84.   E.g. *Printers and Finishers Limited v. Holloway* [1965] 1 W.L.R. 1.
85.   Supra. See: Rideout, *Confidentiality of Protection of Trade Secrets* (1986) 15 I.L.J. 183.
86.   [1987] I.C.R. 464.
87.   [1987] I.R.L.R. 499.
88.   [1984] I.R.L.R. 61.
89.   *Tournier v. National Provincial and Union Bank of England* [1924] 1 K.B. 461 at 463.
90.   [1965] R.P.C. 239.
91.   [1939] 1 All E.R. 290.
92.   *Coco v. A.N. Clarke (Engineers) Limited* [1969] R.P.C. 41.